Grant Edwards

....

SWIMMING +
LESSONS

How to Keep
New Christians Afloat
in a Sinking World

SPECIFICITY

Swimming Lessons: How to Keep New Christians Afloat in a Sinking World

Copyright © Grant Edwards/Specificity Publications

Visit our web site at www.disciplinganother.com

Credits
Copy Editor: Lew Arnold
Designer and Art Director: Barbara Edwards
Cover Art Director: Josh Emrich

Unless otherwise noted, Scripture taken from the HOLY BIBLE, NEW INTERNATIONAL VERSION® . Copyright © 1973, 1978, 1984 by International Bible Society.

All other Scripture taken from the NEW AMERICAN STANDARD BIBLE®, Copyright © 1960,1962,1963,1968,1971,1972,1973,1975,1977 by The Lockman Foundation. Used by permission. (www.Lockman.org)

Contents

Acknowledgments 5

Introduction 7
*Why most churches have all but abandoned discipleship...and how
you can turn that trend around in your church.*

Chapter One: The Soggy Discipler 15
*Wherein I discover discipling – and why before there can be
discipling, there first must be trust.*

Chapter Two: Discipling Begins With You 28
*A chapter in which it becomes clear that discipleship is caught, not
taught, and which will prompt you either to embrace discipleship –
or abandon it.*

Chapter Three: Discipleship and Evangelism. 42
*Where we take one last, long look at what discipleship is and isn't
before we dive into the deep end of the pool.*

Chapter Four: Clearing the Roadblocks 51
*Where we consider the two reasons many people (and churches)
never disciple new believers – and what they can do to overcome
those obstacles.*

Chapter Five: Four Essential Discipling Disciplines. 63
The fundamentals of discipleship that lead to loving Jesus.

Chapter Six: The Essential Discipline of Prayer. 71
Where new disciples learn how to pray – specifically.

Chapter Seven: The Essential Discipline of Bible Study 94
Where new disciples learn what to read in Scripture – specifically.

Chapter Eight: The Essential Discipline of Fellowship 112
Where new disciples form healthy relationships – specifically.

Chapter Nine: The Essential Discipline of Evangelism 127
Where new disciples learn to share their faith — specifically.

Chapter Ten: Three Months That Change Lives. 139
*How and why three months is the ideal time frame for discipling
another to love Jesus.*

Chapter Eleven: Similar Temptations. 153
*Wherein we find there are specific temptations new believers are
likely to encounter…so be prepared.*

Chapter Twelve: One-on-One Culture 164
*Where you'll determine the discipling culture of your church and
consider how shifting to a One-on-One Culture might benefit your
church.*

Chapter Thirteen: Obedience 174
*How the ultimate discipleship discipline — obedience — enabled me to
hear God, make good decisions, and get the girl.*

Chapter Fourteen: Becoming a Discipling Church. 191
*The four steps to becoming a church where discipling happens easily
and naturally.*

A Summary: How to Teach Someone to Swim. 202

Notes 205

Acknowledgments

I have discipled others since I became a Christian over thirty five years ago – this book reflects the lessons and principles of discipleship that I have learned. Any project of time and commitment also takes time and commitment away from those who are close to you.

I could thank many for their commitment and help with this book (which would extend the length to something unreadable). So I need to confine my thanks to my wife Barbara and my children – Megan, Emily, and Matthew. The love and stability in my family makes my ministry and this book possible.

Two friends have shown encouragement and patience for years – John Essig and his wife Elizabeth, along with Bert Barnes and his wife Martha. Thank you.

Rick Ives and Ray Willis continue to plan, work, and direct the work of Discipling Another To Love Jesus. I pray that this book will help our work to restore the lost art of discipleship in local churches.

I have been the pastor of Fellowship Christian Church in Springfield, Ohio for thirty years. The elders, staff, and congregation have prayed, listened, and extended me grace for all of those years.

A year ago I asked a friend from Colorado to help me organize my thoughts for this book. Those thoughts needed a lot more organizing and word-smithing than either of us imagined. Thank you Mikal Keefer for helping to write this book.

During the initial writing I spent a summer at a lake house owned by friend, Monte Zinn. That house was so peaceful it makes me want to go back and write another book.

Introduction

*Why most churches have all but abandoned discipleship
...and how you can turn that trend around in your church.*

Swimming Lessons.

Odd title for a book about making disciples, isn't it?

But think about people you know who've become Christians. At some point they — like you — took a leap of faith and dove into the pool. They're swimming, doing well, growing in their Christian faith.

But others are no longer afloat.

They sank.

You no longer see them attending church. You wonder if they're still in a relationship with God. And no matter what your theology says about their salvation, it's clear they're not having much fun. There's no joy.

Still other people who've taken the plunge seem to constantly struggle in their Christian life. Their heads are above water, but just barely. They move from one faith crisis to another, one series of poor decisions to the next.

What these people need — all of them — are some lessons about how to navigate the water of faith. They need swimming lessons.

Here's the good news: in the same way you can teach someone to swim in water, you can teach someone to hear God, obey him, and thrive in a relationship with him. It's called *discipleship* — and in most churches it's a lost art.

The discipleship litmus test

You remember litmus paper from high school biology? Or was it chemistry? Whatever class it was, litmus paper was *the* way to tell how acidic or basic a liquid was. Your sight might trick you, your sense of smell could be fooled, but place a piece of litmus paper into the test tube and bingo: a no-fail, work-every-time, no-debate-about-it definitive answer.

Here's your litmus paper test about whether you're already prepared to disciple another person to love Jesus.

Answer this question:

If I placed a recently converted Christian into your care, do you know exactly what to do to maximize the chances of this new Christian maturing in Christ?

Don't be ashamed if you can't rattle off your strategy. Most Christians can't because they don't have one. In fact, most *pastors* don't have one.

In the fall of 2002, I was teaching a discipleship conference in the Philippines. In the audience were over 500 pastors and church leaders. I asked them the question I just asked you.

Of the 500 pastors and mature Christians sitting in that room, just ten raised their hands.

Ten.

So let me ask you again:

If I placed a recently converted Christian into your care, do you know what to do to maximize the chances of this new Christian maturing in Christ?

Jot your answer at the top of the next page. Outline your strategy in detail. List the content of what you'd teach and how you'd go about teaching it. Mention what you'd want the new convert to experience. Be as detailed as you can be.

Go ahead...I can wait.

Done?

Here's what I predict: answering this question wasn't as easy as you wish it were. In fact, you might have sidestepped the challenge and kept on reading.

You probably *don't*, in fact, know precisely how to disciple another person to love Jesus. You've got some ideas, but as far as…having a plan…?

It isn't there…yet.

Embracing discipleship

It's not that we're against discipleship. It's right there in the Great Commission, and good luck plowing through the Gospels without tripping over a disciple on every other page. We *support* discipleship — we just don't *do* it.

Instead, we feel guilty. Guilty we're not helping new believers get grounded in their faith. Guilty when we see people join our church and then — within three to six months — fade away and go back to their old lives.

And were we to confess to why we're standing on the discipling sidelines instead of jumping in to help, here are the obstacles most of us would mention:

1. We aren't quite certain how to go about discipling others.
2. Discipling others sounds like an awfully big commitment.

This book addresses both those concerns, and you'll discover that discipling others to love Jesus is something you can do. It's something your entire *church* can do.

I know because for ten years intentional discipleship has changed lives in my church—and in hundreds of churches around the globe that have put this discipleship program in place. I've seen the impact in churches in America, Russia, Cuba, and the Philippines. I've watched programs thrive in suburbs and in prisons.

And soon you'll see the impact of authentic discipleship, too.

In this book I'll tell you everything you need to know to launch effective one-on-one discipling relationships in your church. The approach I'll share is practical, proven, and reproducible.

You'll see new Christians settle into your church and get involved in ministry. Dive into deeper prayer lives. Begin sharing their faith with others. You'll watch older Christians whose enthusiasm for the faith has bordered on "petrified" get excited again.

And you'll soon see these benefits that come with discipleship:

• **Discipleship nails shut the back door of your church.** No more watching new believers walk through the front door and then drift out the back in three or four months. When people connect in discipling relationships, each new believer has a friend at church—one who's actively investing in that new believer's life. Those relationships are like glue; they cause new believers to stick. A Gallup study demonstrated that when someone has a best friend at church, that person is very likely to report high levels of satisfaction with their church. In fact, 87% of church members with a best friend at church gave their church two thumbs up—way up (as reported in the Group/Gallup resource, *Creating a Culture of Connectivity In Your Church*, 2005).[1]

• **Discipleship prompts older believers to remain vibrant in their faith.** Once you've been a Christian for twenty years, you've pretty much heard it all. But when you're sharing faith fundamentals with a new believer, suddenly it's all fresh and exciting again.

• **Discipleship causes growth—in both the disciplers *and* the**

people being discipled. Nothing makes us confront issues in our lives quite like knowing we'll be talking about those issues with someone else. God uses discipling relationships to encourage everyone involved.

And here's one of the most powerful pieces of the discipleship program I'll share with you: once people are discipled, they're trained and set free to disciple others. We encourage each person who goes through the discipling process and training to disciple one person per year—for the rest of their lives. Start doing the multiplication and you'll get a glimpse of the impact discipling will have on your church.

Discipling Another to Love Jesus

We call our program *First Steps*. Every piece of the program is aimed squarely at helping new believers love Jesus.

I'll explain the parts and pieces of the program in the coming chapters, but first, here's a quick example of why it works…

I've been married to Barbara for 30 years, and I'll be the first to admit that I married up. Barbara is beautiful inside and out, through and through. When I decided to marry her, I knew that convincing her to marry me would take some effort. I'll tell you more about that campaign in Chapter Thirteen.

While we were dating, I shifted into Marketing 101: I found out what sort of music she liked and tried to appreciate it. I watched what she ate and did my best to develop a taste for that food. I made changes I hoped would make me more attractive to her.

And my marketing campaign worked.

Then the weirdest thing happened: I discovered that changes I'd made weren't burdens any longer. In fact, they felt natural and normal. As I got to know Barbara better, I wanted to please her, and I began to adopt the behaviors I saw and appreciated in her.

My love for Barbara motivated me to change.

When you love someone and you're in a relationship with him or her, you *want* to make changes that allow the relationship to grow. Nobody *makes* you start picking up your stuff—it just happens. Nobody *forces* you to begin dressing better—you do it because your partner appreciates it.

And it's like that with Jesus. If we love him and spend time with him, we begin assimilating his values and habits. We start doing things that help our relationship with him grow. We become more Christ-like because we *want* to be like him—not because someone is twisting our arm to do the right things.

And that's the goal of discipleship. Not to transmit theology or modify behavior, but to *encourage a loving relationship with Jesus*. All the rest comes later, once a relationship is established.

Keep in mind that when I'm talking about "discipleship" I'm not talking about "evangelism." They're not the same.

Most churches, I've discovered, define "discipleship" as presenting the Gospel and welcoming other people into the Kingdom of God. That's a good thing to do, but it's not discipleship.

Discipleship begins where evangelism leaves off. It's picking up new Christians and helping them become established in the faith, helping them fall in love with Jesus.

The thing that ultimately keeps people involved in Christianity is a relationship with Jesus, not a relationship with doctrine or an institution. If we let new Christians get busy with all sorts of tasks—tithing, working in the nursery, attending small groups—without first cementing that relationship with Jesus, they won't stick around long. And if older Christians drift away from that first love, they'll suffer, too.

Discipling is about relationship…period.

What you'll get from this book

This book is a manifesto of sorts. It gives you an overview of the *First Steps* program, and it's my prayer you'll finish the last chapter with an energizing vision for discipleship. You'll have all the basics and a solid overview of what we've learned over the past ten years about making discipleship a natural part of our church culture.

This book gives you the information and vision, and then I'll tell you where you can get simple tools to put wheels under that vision to get it moving.

Here at *First Steps* we produce discipleship notebooks — a collection of sessions our disciplers use with new believers. They're practical tools that help disciplers remember what to cover and how to go about it. One quick phone call and you can get as many discipleship notebooks as you need.

But frankly, I don't want you to have a discipleship notebooks. Not yet. You'll be tempted to dive into a discipling program without the background you'll get in *Swimming Lessons,* and I can predict what will happen.

Within six months the notebooks will be sitting on a shelf in the church office. Or tossed in the backseat of your car.

What you need *now* — and what you're about to get — is a desire to move into a risky, power-packed adventure that literally changes lives. To grab hold of a vision for discipleship.

Oh — and here's a bonus for you

Stick with me until the end of this book, and I'll also teach you to swim.

Honest.

If you've got access to a pool, you're going to put down this book knowing everything you need to know to start swimming or to teach someone else to swim. You'll be ready to go.

No kidding.

Well, *almost* ready. Don't jump into ten feet of water holding this book and expect to start doing laps if you're terrified of the water. While you'll have all the knowledge you need to become a competent swimmer, you still need someone to help you get started.

And exactly the same thing is true of discipleship.

You see, just like swimming, *discipleship was never intended to happen alone.* All the read-the-Bible-in-one-year programs in the world won't truly disciple a young believer. Neither will listening to sermons, doing daily devotions, or watching the *Jesus* film for the umpteenth time. They're helpful, but they're not discipleship.

Some of those believers you've seen sink were doing all those things, plus tithing. And all those good activities didn't save them because they didn't get the most important stuff right.

There are basic, fundamental, faith-building disciplines that help us know and love Jesus — and we almost certainly can't learn them on our own. It just doesn't happen. So unless you're intentional about building discipleship relationships in your church, it's as if you have handed non-swimming new believers a Bible and shoved them off the diving board into deep water.

They have all the information they need in hand. And they'll have it in hand the entire time they're drifting to the bottom of the pool, where they'll promptly drown. Information isn't enough.

That's why we put *First Steps* in place at our church. We were tired of watching new Christians fade away when they failed to fall in love with Jesus. We were tired of watching Christians who'd been around awhile stop growing, or even worse — turn into modern-day Pharisees who were big on rules but who didn't have a heart for God.

Are you tired of those same things? Want to feel a new vitality and excitement blow through your church and your own life?

Then get ready for an adventure.

Pull on your goggles — we're diving in.

1

~~~~

The Soggy Discipler

Wherein I discover discipling — and why before
there can be discipling, there first must be trust.

My own adventure with discipling others was launched at the least likely time of my life and in the least likely place.

I wasn't yet a Christian ... and I was standing in a swimming pool.

You see, during my high school years, I spent summers teaching inner-city kids to swim. I worked for an Ohio agency, and every two weeks we'd set up a portable pool on a different school playground. These schools had no pools, so most of the kids who enrolled in our two-week "swim camp" had absolutely no clue about how to stay afloat.

The first year I did my best — but lots of kids left the program exactly as they'd entered: terrified of the water and sinking like rocks. I'd tried, they'd tried, but there was no success.

Then I discovered something.

I realized kids weren't failing because they were afraid of drowning or afraid of the water. They weren't even afraid of looking silly in front of their friends. None of that was even on their sonar screens.

What they feared was the *unknown*. Kids were terrified they'd lose control, be unable to breathe, and have no idea what to do as they drifted toward the bottom of the pool.

Scared kids get stiff as a board. But unlike boards, which naturally *float*, stiff kids naturally *sink*. Fear paralyzes beginning swimmers.

To overcome their fear, the kids needed someone to take control. To inspire confidence. They needed someone they could trust.

So I tried something new. Before I allowed kids into the pool I lined them up and I kneeled down so we were eye-to-eye. I said, "If you want to learn to swim, there are just two things you need to do. Just two, so listen close.

"First, follow my instructions.

"Second, *trust me*. I'm not going to let you drown."

I repeated my instructions several times until I got nods of agreement.

Once kids looked me in the eye and decided to trust me, they'd taken the first step in learning to swim — before they even got their toes wet. Their trust let them relax and be unafraid as they slipped into the water.

Within 30 minutes I had all the kids floating. Within an hour I had them all swimming.

Nobody would mistake these new swimmers for Olympians, but they could make it from one end of the pool to the other. And as those kids finished their first lap, grinning up from the water, you'd think they'd all won gold medals.

They were thrilled — and so was I.

"*Trust me.*" Those were the words that had mattered most. Once kids trusted me and followed my instructions, they quickly mastered what had seemed impossible. And nobody drowned.

"*Trust me.*"

I had no idea how important those words would become in my life.

The bumbling discipler

Fast forward a few years and I was in the ministry…sort of.

I graduated from high school in 1971 and then did what way too many other young people did back then: I left home and lived on the road. While I wasn't making good choices in general, I *did* understand the concept of snow, so by the end of December I was in Daytona Beach.

It's there I ran into some Christians who were active in the Jesus Movement. And on New Year's Eve, 1971, I accepted Jesus as my Lord.

Cranked up with a new sense of purpose (and short on money), I headed back to Ohio, where I started sharing my faith with friends and other young people I met. Within three months nearly a hundred of those people confessed Christ.

So there I was: three months old as a Christian and looking at a flock of one hundred — each of those young sheep looking back at me for guidance. None of us realized exactly how much trouble we were in.

My success in helping those new Christians mature and thrive was — at best — dismal. I'd lead someone to Christ and then watch the person walk right back into old patterns, old sins, old life.

People were *coming* to Christ, but very few of them actually *stuck* with him. Our little fellowship, meeting in basements around town, had a revolving door that just wouldn't close. People came; people left. Few stayed.

I realized I needed to learn what caused new Christians to grow in Christ, what would help them get grounded during their first months in the faith. And I needed the information *fast.*

For three months I started my mornings with Bible study and prayer, always with one focus: *What does it take for a new Christian to grow in Christ?*

I read every book I could find on Christian growth. I started attending a Bible college, and I asked a professor to write and submit a term paper to *me* outlining what it took for new Christians to mature. To his credit, the professor did as I asked.

I was desperate, sinking, letting everyone down. If there's no greater joy than seeing someone come to know Jesus as a result of your efforts, there's no greater frustration than watching that same person walk away from faithfulness.

I was missing something…something important.

But what was it?

Trust and the art of staying afloat

One day, while having lunch with an experienced pastor in town, I expressed my frustrations. He listened, nodded, and then said something that changed my life.

"The Great Commission is not about evangelism; it's about discipleship," Pastor John said. "You have to win and then *disciple* the lost."

This was news to me. I'd been all about winning the lost. Who knew there was a second step to the process?

Trying not to sound completely ignorant, I asked, "So…what's discipleship?"

Pastor John learned forward. He said, "A new Christian can't make it alone. Discipleship is a one-on-one relationship. A new Christian has to listen to and follow someone who will show that new believer how to grow. Someone trustworthy."

There it was again—that word *trust.*

It hit me: the same lesson I'd learned about growing swimmers held true in growing new Christians. I was right back on the edge of the pool. *"Trust me"* were still the two words that opened the door to risky, significant growth.

Except this time we weren't talking about learning to dog-paddle. This time we were talking about learning to live.

Swimming lesson #1

There are several things we swimming instructors know that new swimmers don't know — and the first is the power of relationship.

I've already mentioned the importance of trust, and maybe you brushed it aside. Don't. Trust is absolutely critical when facing beginning swimmers. They must trust that you know what you're doing as an instructor — and that you care about them.

And here's the second secret: to float on their stomachs swimmers must stretch out and relax. Seems simple, doesn't it?

But stretching out and relaxing are *not* natural responses for new swimmers. Put new swimmers face down in water and almost always they bend their knees and draw their legs up under themselves. They feel more protected that way, more natural.

But all those fledgling swimmers accomplish is to turn their bodies into balls. Bowling balls. Bowling balls that sink.

Growing as a swimmer requires doing things that feel counter-intuitive. Things that make perfect sense to the instructor but that new swimmers find scary and uncomfortable. Things new swimmers won't try until they decide to trust their instructor and accept their instructor's directions.

When I was working with children who feared the water, here's how that process played out…

I'd hold a child's hand and say, "Let me pull you around the pool." I'd then slowly pull the kid around and around the pool in lazy circles. As we moved I'd say, "Relax. Let your legs stretch out behind you. I'm not going to let you go. Trust me."

Before long, my swimming student began listening, following my instructions, and trusting me. He'd relax.

Then came the next step. As I continued pulling I'd say, "Lower your face into the water. Hold your breath while I pull you." Again I'd circle the pool several times as the child lowered and raised his face.

By this time the child was actually floating but didn't know it. If I could let go and the kid didn't tense up by lifting his head or drawing up his legs, he'd float. He'd be fine.

But he didn't *know* he'd be okay. He needed to discover that he'd stay afloat after I let go...but what would convince him of that?

One thing and one thing only: trust.

I'd say, "Listen, I've pulled you awhile and you aren't hurt. You haven't drowned. I'm right here with you and I can touch bottom. Plus, I'm a good swimmer and I'm watching out for you.

"Now I want you to put your head in the water and hold your breath. Then, as I'm pulling you, I'll let you go for a few seconds. Stay relaxed and keep your head in the water. I'll be right beside you. After a few seconds I'll grab your hands again, and then you can lift your head."

I then let go, just for a few seconds. Almost always the child would float along calmly until I did what I promised I'd do: hold his hands again. Then he'd lift his head and flash me a smile.

He'd floated for the first time.

Had I taught that child to float? Yes...but not until I'd taught him to listen to me and trust that I was on his side. Convinced him he wasn't alone in the water. Won his confidence that I'd see him through the process until he was a safe, capable swimmer.

That's the same sort of trust new Christians need to have in their disciplers—and the same level of involvement a discipler needs to have in the life of someone he or she is discipling.

Notice that I *earned* the trust of the children I was teaching. I wasn't offended they didn't automatically trust me. They were scared and in a completely new environment—of *course* they tested me to see if I was trustworthy. I'd have done the same thing. So would you.

I earned children's trust by being clear about what I was doing and why I was doing it. I encouraged them. And even more importantly, *I got in the pool with them.* Had I tried to teach without getting wet, they wouldn't have learned.

You earn trust by demonstrating competence in what you're attempting to teach, but that's just part of it. You also earn trust by jumping in the pool yourself to come alongside a new swimmer.

A good swimming instructor always smells just a bit like chlorine. And a good discipler usually looks as if he or she has recently been in prayer.

Swimming lesson # 2

When learning to swim, beginners do as you do — *not* as you say. They need the reassurance of having you beside them, demonstrating good technique.

I know there are elite swim coaches who show up to practice wearing polo shirts and carrying clipboards, who conduct the entire practice from the side of the pool. They never get wet.

But that's not what coaches of *new* swimmers do. New swimmers — and new Christians — need the reassurance of seeing the coach in the water. That's where the trust is built.

When trust evaporates

Compare how I taught children to swim with what a friend of mine experienced when her father decided it was time she mastered the water.

Tricia can't remember how old she was — five or six — when she saw her father standing chest deep in a lake at the end of a dock.

"He told me to jump in and held his arms out to catch me. He'd always caught me before, so I trusted him completely. I stepped back, got a running start, and leapt, reaching out to him. That's when to my horror my Daddy stepped aside and let me cannonball into the water — which was over my head."

Tricia gasped for breath as she sank beneath the dark water. She panicked, struggling to find the surface, sucking in a deep gulp of water. That's when her father reached down and pulled her up to safety.

"I know he was trying to teach me to swim," she says. "I was underwater for what—five seconds? But here's the thing: I'm a grown woman and I *still* can't swim. After that experience I could never get back into the water. My father didn't teach me to swim—he taught me to not trust him."

Ouch.

Was that what I'd done when I helped friends become Christians and then moved on, not helping them as they desperately struggled to stay afloat? Had my enthusiasm for moving along to do more evangelism left friends to drown? I'd convinced them to jump in by holding my arms out to them—but I hadn't caught them and coached them how to survive in the new environment of faith.

And here's a question for you: *Is that what you're doing?*

If your ministry isn't characterized by intentional discipling of believers—especially new ones—let me encourage you to do this: count the bodies you see floating around you.

- Tally up the members of your church whose attendance has become occasional, then sporadic, then stopped altogether.

- Count the new believers who've never quite plugged into the ministries of your church. They're around—but they aren't growing in their faith.

- Do the math as you review the church roster: how many of your church members have led someone to the Lord in the past year?

- How wide open is the back door to *your* ministry? Are people drifting out of your church as fast (or faster) than they're coming in through the front door?

My goal isn't for you to feel guilty. That won't help.

Instead, I want you to see what I saw: that unless we disciple new believers, getting them firmly rooted in the Christian faith, it's as if we're tossing them into the deep end of a pool and hoping they'll find a way to stay afloat.

Here's what's strange: there *are* people who learn to swim by being tossed in deep water. They don't win any points for style, but somehow they keep their heads above water.

And these people *love* to tell you all about how they toughed it out, how they overcame the odds. They figure if they made it, everyone can make it. And if you listen long enough, it begins to make sense. Why not put people in challenging situations and force them to depend on God and themselves?

Because it's a terrible idea, that's why.

Keep in mind those people with the great stories are the survivors. Theirs are the only voices being heard. The vast majority of people — the ones who struggled and then drowned — aren't lining up to do interviews.

If a few people survive and become swimmers when thrown into deep water, does that make "dock-tossing" the preferred method for swimming instruction? It's an easy approach for us swimming instructors; all we have to do is bury the bodies that wash up on shore.

If a few new Christians continue to stand strong when tossed back into their daily lives without discipling, does that make "Christian-tossing" the preferred method for helping believers grow in their faith? It's an easy approach for us church leaders; all we have to do is scratch our heads and wonder why people today can't make a commitment and see it through.

I'm going out on a limb here: I'm betting you're a Christian who survived even though you were never formally discipled. I'm playing the odds: you're reading a discipleship book (so you're established in your faith) and I know from experience that few churches do programs like *First Steps*.

But don't get cocky: I'd also bet that even if you were never intentionally discipled, God still brought a discipler or two into your life.
Somewhere an older Christian took an interest in you and invested in
your spiritual growth. Maybe you got encouragement and coaching
from a Sunday school teacher, parent, or even a peer who was a bit
farther down the faith path than you.

Those disciplers helped you know and love Jesus.

And they kept you from drowning.

Trustworthy discipleship

I want to be very clear: discipleship matters. In the long run, I
believe it's the primary difference between Christians who thrive,
leading joyful, purposeful Kingdom lives—and those who either fade
away or who simply limp along waiting for Heaven.

Consider the words and example of Jesus. Discipleship of new believers isn't optional—it's mandatory. Unfortunately, it seldom happens in an intentional, organized way.

The power of *First Steps* is that it addresses the most important
things a believer needs to know and do, and does so in the context of a
one-on-one relationship. People who've known Jesus awhile climb in
the water with new believers to make sure that new Christians don't
just know *about* Jesus—they *know Jesus.*

And by "new Christians" I don't mean just new converts.

I'm no child psychologist, but I have two daughters and a son, so
I've lived in a developmental lab for the past twenty years. I can tell
you with some authority that there are stages children move through
developmentally.

One of those stages is what we Dads of Daughters describe as the
"discovering boys" stage.

I know fathers whose daughters first noticed boys at the age of
ten or eleven. I know other dads whose daughters looked up from a
textbook or swim club or mission trip when they were in college and

wham—they saw boys. And boys saw them.

My daughters didn't go through every stage on the same schedule, and that's fine. God wired them differently. And frankly, the longer they cared more about ponies than prom dresses, the happier I was.

But all along I knew that, eventually, I wanted my son and both my girls to be happily married and serving God in the context of fulfilling marriages. I know what my marriage with Barbara has given me through the years, and I can't think of anything more precious for my children.

I also knew my girls wouldn't get to the "fulfilled marriage" stage until they got through the "discovering boys" stage. That's just how it works. First things first.

But I didn't have to like it.

There are also stages in the Christian life that you can't get to until you go through other stages first. It's not a function of how old you are, or how long you've been a believer—it's whether you've matured.

Intentional discipleship is a powerful way to be sure that growth happens because believers are planted where it *can* happen—in a loving relationship with Jesus.

 SINK OR SWIM QUESTIONS

In each chapter we'll pause to consider the "so what" ramifications of the previous pages. Consider this the application portion of the book, and you skip these chances to ponder at your own risk.

Why is moving past these questions dangerous?

Because the goal of discipleship isn't information—it's *transformation*. That's what being in the presence of a living God does: it changes you. It *transforms* you. That's why when you disciple another person to love Jesus, it's primarily about relationship, not theology.

And that's my goal with you here. I'll give you an outline for initiating a discipleship program in your church. You'll know precisely how to answer the discipleship litmus test question.

If I placed a recently converted Christian into your care — realizing there's a strong possibility that the new believer will walk away from faithfulness during the first three months — do you know what to do to maximize the chances of this new Christian maturing in Christ?

You'll get information about how to set up a discipleship program — but that's not the primary purpose of this book.

The primary purpose is to see you *transformed*. I want you to let God speak to you about the importance of discipling others to love Jesus, and that won't happen if you rush through this book as if you have a book report due tomorrow morning.

So slow down. Take your time. Think. Pray.

And let me suggest this, too: if you're currently in a discipling relationship with someone, get hold of another copy of this book and read together with your discipler. Work through the chapters and questions together. See if they resonate in your experience together.

Assessment time

- *How intentional is your church about discipling?*

- *What systematic programs do you have in place to assure that discipling happens?*

Slightly uncomfortable assessment time

- *How intentional are you personally about discipling others?*

- *Who have you discipled in the past year?*

Massively uncomfortable assessment time

- *Who discipled you?*

- *What benefits do you think might have been realized in your life had you been discipled in a systematic way?*

- And the question that gets right to the heart of the matter: *If I placed a recently converted Christian into your care — realizing there's a strong possibility that new believer will walk away from faithfulness during the first three months — do you know what to do to maximize the chances of this new Christian maturing in Christ?*

Prayer

Dear God, yours is a Kingdom of transformation, and we want to be part of it. And we want to cooperate with your desire to see others around us transformed, too. Give us eyes to see how discipleship plays a part in bringing others to you. Amen.

2

~~~~

Discipling Begins With You

*A chapter in which it becomes clear that discipleship is
caught, not taught, and which will prompt you either to
embrace discipleship – or abandon it.*

One morning when I was about twelve, I opened the morning paper and saw something that iced my blood.

Splashed across the front page was a photograph of my friend, Frank. Frank was sitting on the bank of a pond. I recognized the location—it was in a city park near my house.

In the photograph Frank's clothes were soaked, clinging to his lean frame. His hair was matted to his forehead, and on his face was a look of complete and total despair.

Two things struck me: first, Frank must still be alive or there wouldn't be a picture of him. That was the good news.

And second, Frank shouldn't have been wet. There was no swimming in that pond—everyone knew that. The water was murky and cold, the bottom of the pond choked with weeds. There was even a sign posted to warn people to stay out of the water.

The article spelled out what had happened in a few brief paragraphs.

The day before, as Frank was walking past the pond, he'd seen a boy in the water. The boy was struggling, paddling furiously but unable to stay afloat. Frank kicked off his shoes, ran into the pond, and swam quickly to where the boy had disappeared beneath the dark water.

Frank tried to save the boy, but it was too late.

A newspaper reporter had tried to interview Frank, but what was there to say? He'd done too little, arrived too late. The unnamed swimmer was dead.

The photograph captured Frank's defeat perfectly.

The thing is, Frank was *exactly* the right guy to attempt a rescue. He was a strong, experienced swimmer. He was like a fish in the water. He knew lifesaving like the back of his hand.

I'd met Frank at the YMCA, where we'd both been on the swim team. Frank had invited me to join the Aquatic Leader's Club, and that's where I got hooked on teaching others to swim.

Frank was quite the recruiter. He convinced more than a dozen of us to join, and each of Frank's recruits taught hundreds of kids how to stay alive in deep water. It's not a stretch to say that through Frank's efforts thousands of children learned to swim.

But none of it mattered that day in the park.

Swimming lesson #3

The boy who jumped in the pond and tried to make it across was clearly enthusiastic about swimming. But being enthusiastic and being prepared are two completely different things. His enthusiasm couldn't sustain him all the way to the far shore.

In addition to coaching swimming, I've also coached basketball. There are lots of differences between those sports, but the biggest one is this: nobody has ever drowned playing basketball.

Today, on courts and in driveways, there are thousands of beginning basketball players trying to perfect a lay-up or a fade-away three-pointer. And for at least the first hundred times they try, they're awful. The ball bangs off the rim, or lands on the roof, or ricochets through a storm window. But other than perhaps spraining an ankle or suffering a deflated ego, there's no danger to the kids learning to play.

Not so with swimming.

Make a mistake when you're learning to swim and you can literally die. The enthusiasm and self-confidence that leads a beginner to take a leap off the high dive is the same enthusiasm that will get him killed.

We swim coaches have to walk a fine line: we want to instill confidence, but not *suicidal* confidence. That's why there are so many rules for swimmers.

It's why you need a swim buddy. Why, unless you're a truly experienced swimmer, you need to swim where there's a lifeguard watching. Why you have to keep a sharp eye on the current and swim conditions.

The young man pulled out of that pond was a beginner who never got the chance to get better; his enthusiasm took his life. He hadn't paid attention to one of the most worn, faded, and ignored pieces of advice a swim instructor can give: *don't get in over your head.*

That simply means this: don't get into situations that are beyond your skill level. Don't assume that dedication alone will save you. It takes developed skills, too.

How do you know when you're ready to swim a lap or to cross the English Channel? Simple—your swimming instructor will tell you.

And your instructor will be nearby when you make the attempt. Just like your discipler.

I talked with Frank later. Frank shook his head and said, "If that kid had been a member of the 'Y,' we would have taught him to swim, wouldn't we?"

I nodded. It was true—that kid was *exactly* like the kids we helped.

But because Frank hadn't reached him in time, the boy had perished.

From that day forward, Frank had a new mission as a swim instructor: he was going to see to it that every child in the world learned to swim. All of them. Everywhere. Somehow, some way, he was going to make it happen.

Has Frank been successful?

Not yet...but it's not for a lack of focus or effort.

Maybe Frank's sort of passion for bringing the whole world along feels familiar to you. It does to me — it's exactly how I felt when I first became a believer and noticed nearly all my enthusiastic friends were drowning spiritually — whether they knew it or not. I wanted to jump into the pond and pull as many as possible to safety. And I knew exactly where I wanted to start: with my best friend, Mike.

A mission to Mike

From the first day of kindergarten through high school graduation and beyond, Mike was my best friend. We were inseparable, like two brothers who just happened to live in different houses. Good times, tough times, everything from learning to read to learning to drive — we experienced all of it together.

I was raised in a Christian home and Mike wasn't, but since I didn't care about Jesus, the whole religious thing didn't create any conflict between us. We were on the same page as we became co-conspirators in the discovery of sports, girls, parties, drinking, and drugs.

Here's how it usually worked. Mike would suggest something so dangerous or outrageous that I immediately vetoed the idea — I wasn't interested in going to jail.

Then, after pondering the logistics, I'd figure out a way we *might* be able to pull it off, maybe. I'd lay out my plan to Mike, and presto — we were in business. Between his ideas and my scheming, we made a great team. Name any temptation you might encounter in high school, and Mike and I figured out a way to climb aboard.

We thought we were getting away with it. And we *were*—for awhile.

Then came the moment the consequences of my sin began returning more pain than pleasure. I saw myself for who I really was: a prodigal who needed to find his way home to a forgiving father.

A gracious God welcomed me back, and my salvation snatched me from the jaws of addiction. I was overjoyed about my new life in Jesus and wanted to tell everyone I knew what God had done for me.

Starting with Mike.

To my amazement, Mike accepted Jesus as his Lord and Savior, too. The dynamic duo was back in action, but this time we were serving God.

One year out of high school, with all the enthusiasm of new converts, we pondered what to do next. Mike suggested we convert all of our friends and acquaintances. Isn't that what Christians did?

Well, yes, but…you had to consider how many *people* we knew (lots) and how *little* we knew (next to nothing) and what we should say to people (we had no idea)….

Mike sat quietly as I thought and schemed. Then the plan came into focus for me. We'd just tell people what Jesus did for us, who Jesus is, and ask people to sign up. And figuring it would take awhile to get to everyone we knew, we had to get started right away. And to hold the harvest, we'd also start what was then known as a "Jesus House," a bunch of Christian guys living together and winning others. It'd be our ministry.

No time to waste.

Keep in mind this was less than *two weeks* after I'd become a Christian. I knew nothing about sermon preparation. I knew next to nothing about Scripture. All I knew was that I'd been such an evangelist for evil—convincing many of my high school friends to abuse alcohol and drugs—that I thought it necessary to share with them something truly worth sharing: Jesus.

I invited 16 of my friends to get together with me at a friend's apartment, and all 16 came. Since I didn't know what else to do, I simply shared my testimony. Then I asked if any of my friends would also like to become Christians.

All 16 people in attendance raised their hands.

Later my mentor, Pastor John, approached me and put his arm around my shoulders. He said, "Grant, remember that there's no greater feeling, nothing more exciting, than seeing God work through you to impact the life of another person."

John's statement has echoed in my life ever since — because he was absolutely right. One of discipleship's greatest blessings is that new believers get a proper foundation for a lifetime of faithfully loving and serving Jesus. But there's another blessing, too.

It's that we disciplers have a tremendously fulfilling ministry.

We're empowered to share eternal truths and speak into the lives of people God made and loves. We're empowered to make a difference — and that empowerment brings so much joy into the lives of disciplers.

Empowered...but ineffective

My initial evangelism efforts were remarkably effective. Within three months more than one hundred teenagers we knew became Christians. They're the little flock I mentioned earlier. They prayed the prayer, bought Bibles, and started talking about God. Everything was sunshine and testimonies.

But then came the tough stuff of life: living out a new faith in the same relationships where they'd been heathens. Confronting temptation. Enduring ridicule. Realizing that this was a long-term, everyday proposition, a total commitment.

As I've already described, most of the hundred new believers didn't endure. One at a time they walked away from Jesus. They disappeared from our fellowship and drifted back into their old lives.

Then one day Mike was gone as well.

I was devastated. My best friend had crossed back into the shadows. What was I going to do?

And how could I keep such a wholesale migration from happening again? I needed help; and there wasn't a book (I bought them all), a seminar (I even tried seminary), or a class that could help me. Praying, fasting, imploring God for answers—nothing worked.

Well, almost nothing.

Pastor John to the rescue

Many of God's most impressive miracles have nothing to do with flash and sizzle—no multiplying loaves, no splitting the air with thunderbolts, or no erasing Egyptian armies.

The miracles are small. Unnoticed. Yet they're powerful beyond measure.

God worked one of those miracles in my life when he brought an older, wiser pastor into my life. A pastor with a heart to spend time with me.

A pastor who could *disciple* me.

Let me be clear: God knew I needed time with Pastor John. I knew nothing, and it seemed to me Pastor John knew everything. I could ask John anything, and he'd patiently listen, ask a few questions, and then deliver a hefty dose of wisdom.

I know *now* that I was being discipled as a leader and a Christ-follower, but I didn't know that then. At the time I just knew I'd found an older friend who had insights to share, and who seemed to understand my life.

I wonder if the apostles truly understood that they were being discipled by Jesus. As I read the New Testament, I see nothing about the twelve being lined up and officially sworn into Jesus' Traveling School of Apostle Preparation.

Their experience was simply this: they wanted to be with Jesus, and he wanted them to follow him. Jesus set the agenda and the apostles tagged along, learning by watching Jesus, hearing and discussing his teaching.

Sort of like how I was learning by watching and listening to Pastor John.

I told John about Mike and our friendship, our early years, and how we'd become brothers in the faith. Then I shared that Mike had forsaken following Jesus and what a bitter disappointment that was for me.

John listened quietly, and when I had finished rambling, he looked at me over his glasses.

"Grant," he said, "why are you telling me this?"

That wasn't a question I'd expected. I'd just poured out my *soul* to this man, and he was asking me why I'd done it? Still, John's questions usually had a point, so I answered as honestly as I could.

"Because I respect and trust you," I said.

John nodded thoughtfully. "One of the most difficult things you'll face as a pastor is watching people walk away from Jesus," he said. "It happens all the time, and I guess it shouldn't be a surprise. Jesus himself said that many of the Gospel seeds planted would quickly sprout and then wilt because they didn't take root properly."

John shifted in his chair and leaned in, the way he always did when he was about to say something important.

"You say you respect and trust me, but there's something else going on between us. I've been a pastor for more than forty years, and when we talk you hope you'll glean something you can use in your ministry. That's fine—I enjoy mentoring you.

But you're not just *listening* to me, Grant. You're *watching* me, too. You're weighing what I say and do against the teachings of Jesus. And if you see or hear something inconsistent, you'll lose respect for me at once. You won't want to listen to me any longer.

Our friendship is helpful to you because I've already gone many of the places you want to go, both spiritually and professionally. I'm talking from experience. I can point the way because I know the lay of the land.

You want to see new Christians become deeply rooted in the faith, to flower and bring forth fruit. As you grow in experience as a believer and a pastor, you'll learn some techniques to help that happen. God will give you that desire of your heart because it's a desire of *his* heart.

But no discipling technique, teaching, or program can replace what's most important: *you being a true disciple yourself.*

If there's a secret, it's this: no student is greater than his teacher. If you want others to follow Jesus, show them how by following Jesus yourself. If you want others to bear fruit, show them where to plant themselves so they can grow by planting yourself there first."

Pastor John knew what the Apostle Paul knew: that discipleship is caught, not taught. Like Frank's infectious enthusiasm for swimming had turned me from an occasional splasher into a serious swimmer, my enthusiasm for God could influence others.

But Frank hadn't just inspired me—he'd trained me, too.

He'd *discipled* me.

And I needed to disciple others.

When Paul wrote to the Corinthians, "Follow my example, as I follow the example of Christ" (1 Corinthians 11:1), Paul pretty much defined what discipleship looks like. It's a game of follow the leader— and the one setting the pace and defining the path is Jesus himself.

Jesus said that his very food was to do the will of the Father (John 4:34). In doing what God wanted, Jesus healed the sick, set the captives free, and preached the good news to the lost. He performed miracles, lived simply, ministered to the poor, and died on a cross.

Jesus was perfect—and perfectly did the will of God.

Paul most certainly *wasn't* perfect, but as he followed the example of Jesus, he lived sacrificially, healed the sick, preached to the Gentiles, and allowed the Holy Spirit to guide his writing to the extent that those letters to churches have been included in the New Testament.

As imperfect as Paul was, he discipled others by word, example, and pointing toward Jesus. He was faithful in sharing what he knew, and he expected those he influenced to influence others.

Paul wrote to Timothy, "And the things you have heard me say in the presence of many witnesses entrust to reliable men who will also be qualified to teach others" (2 Timothy 2:2).

Now, be sure you hear what I'm *not* saying. I'm *not* saying that you should try to mimic everything Paul did. For instance, you might want to avoid shipwrecks unless they're absolutely necessary. You probably don't have the same gifts or skills Paul had. God clearly doesn't need to send another believer to Rome to stand trial before Caesar.

The goal isn't to be a copycat. The goal is to be intentional in knowing, loving, and following Jesus — and teaching others to do the same.

How will that look in your life? I'm not sure. I do know there will be some fundamentals (more about them later) that will look pretty much like they've always looked. But everything else?

That's between you and God.

Here's what I *do* know, though; every Christian can follow the example of Jesus and Paul in learning to disciple others. Discipleship is a bit what you know, but it's even more your decision to be available. To decide to let God use you.

Unless you're living alone in a cave, in fact, you're *already* modeling the faith for anyone who knows you. For better or worse, you're communicating what it is to be a believer. There are people watching you, being influenced by how you live. You simply cannot opt out of influencing others.

But will you *embrace* your role as a discipler? Will you risk investing in the lives of others to help establish them in the Kingdom?

If so, know that you're desperately needed—because there aren't a lot of Christians making the commitment to disciple others intentionally and well. Don't believe me? Then consider what George Barna, a leading Christian sociologist and pollster, discovered when he did extensive research into the spiritual lives of teenagers and adults who report they've made a personal commitment to Jesus.

In his book *Growing True Disciples,* Barna reports that when Christian adults were asked to identify their most important goal for their lives, not a single person said it was to be a committed follower of Jesus Christ or to make disciples of Christ.1

Not one.

Not a single person said that the most important goal of his life was to be a committed follower of Jesus *or to make disciples of Christ.* The Great Commission was given to all Christians, but few of us have as a goal to disciple another to love and obey Jesus.

So are you needed as a discipler? You betcha.

If you're willing to disciple another person, take a look at the Sink or Swim questions below.

If you're not willing, take a look at the *other* Sink or Swim questions below.

It's time either to get in the pool or hit the showers.

Before you decide which set of questions to answer

It's usually the last words that matter most. That's where we often say what's closest to our hearts.

At the family reunion it's when Cousin Sara is sitting in her car, leaning out through the window to share a few last words with her favorite relatives, that she says, "I love you."

It's when the front door is hanging open and my grown children are pulling on their coats to leave that I get in one last word with them. I give them a hug and a kiss and remind them that I'm proud of them. I know no matter what else we talked about earlier, it's those parting words that are remembered longest.

When I was in junior high school, a friend lost his mother to cancer. She called him to her bedside as she was dying and prayed for him. He later told me she'd encouraged him to be faithful to Jesus.

That was a long time ago, and he's spent his life working as a disc jockey, playing songs and listening to callers. His business is words... and I know he's never forgotten those last words he heard from his mother.

Jesus shared some last words, too.

He asked his disciples to meet him in Galilee. That was an 80-mile, four-day walk away, and when the disciples showed up, they must have been expecting some significant announcement to justify the trip.

If that was the case, they were disappointed. Matthew records Jesus' words, and he really didn't say all that much.

> *All authority in heaven and on earth has been given to me. Therefore go and make disciples of all nations, baptizing them in the name of the Father and of the Son and of the Holy Spirit, and teaching them to obey everything I have commanded you. And surely I am with you always, to the very end of the age.* — Matthew 28:18-20

Question: why did the apostles have to walk 80 miles, then turn around and walk 80 miles back, just to hear that? Jesus could have given those instructions anywhere. But these were last words. Important words. Words Jesus wanted to be sure his disciples would never forget.

The walk to and from Galilee provided two spectacular opportunities: four days to anticipate what Jesus was going to say, and then four days to think about what he actually had said.

And Jesus' words were never forgotten: *"Therefore go and make disciples."*

Marching orders for the disciples. Marching orders for us. Marching orders for you.

 SINK OR SWIM QUESTIONS

If you're willing to disciple others...

- *Why do you think Jesus put such an emphasis on discipleship?*

- *What benefits might your church realize if new church members were discipled in a systematic, intentional way?*

- *What obstacles do you think you might encounter if you try to put a systematic discipleship program in place at your church?*

Prayer

Dear God, thank you for the privilege of introducing others to you, for your guidance in the process and the joy that's coming as we follow you. Bring into our lives people we can disciple and who can disciple us. Amen.

 SINK OR SWIM QUESTIONS

If you're unwilling to disciple others...

- *What is it about discipling that you find distasteful?*

- *What negative thing or things might happen in your church if discipleship were a part of your culture?*

- *If you were convinced Jesus wants you to be discipled or to disciple others, would you be willing? What would it take to convince you?*

Prayer

Dear God, sometimes what you ask of us feels too hard. We don't have a vision for what you're trying to accomplish or a heart for what you want to do. Give me a heart for discipleship if it's what you really want to do in and through me. Give me a vision for what discipleship can do in and through me.   Amen.

3

~~~~

Discipleship and Evangelism

*Where we take one last, long look at what discipleship is
and isn't before we dive into the deep end of the pool.*

Have you ever walked along the beach in Florida or Southern California and noticed the lifeguard towers?

They're the wooden boxes sitting up on stilts, and on television there's always a tall, bronzed surfer-dude perched up there in a chair, watching the water through $200 sunglasses. At least once — usually just before a commercial — you see the lifeguard spring into action because way out there, barely visible, a swimmer is struggling to stay afloat.

The lifeguard leaps from the twenty-foot tower and sprints toward the water, hauling a floatation board behind him. He dives beneath the first wave and surfaces to race like a torpedo to the gasping victim. And on the spot he revives a drowning beauty queen, frees a whale, pets a dolphin, and dope-slaps a shark, all at once.

Lifeguards are like that. At least, the ones on *television* are like that.

In *real* life, the coolest thing about being a lifeguard — other than the low pay and opportunity to develop skin cancer — is the possibility to one day be a hero. To one day have all your training and physical conditioning pay off. To one day leap into action (by carefully climbing down from the tower, thank you; nobody needs a lifeguard with a broken leg) and do some good.

And it almost never happens.

Most lifeguards I know have never pulled someone to safety. They toot whistles as a warning when someone is about to do something dumb, and they teach a lot of swimming classes.

But save lives? Nope.

Does that mean that a lifeguard's role is useless? That every day he or she drives home after a shift without rescuing someone was a wasted day?

Of course not. If a lifeguard is doing the job well, that lifeguard will keep situations on the side of the pool or on the beach from turning into problems in the water. A lifeguard will watch to see that nobody drifts out too far from the shore or dog-paddles into water that's too deep. A lifeguard will keep "wrestling in the water" from becoming "drowning after being held under too long by an idiot friend."

Lifeguards can be effective even if they're never awarded a lifesaving medal by the mayor. Saving lives is just one part of the job.

In the church, we're often trained to think like lifeguards when it comes to evangelism. We're told our friends and acquaintances are being swept out to sea and it's our job to get them safely to land. Our efforts are heroic, epic even, as time after time we leap into action and drag the drowning to shore.

It's almost as if we've got our own theme music.

I've got nothing against rescuing the lost, but there's a problem. Next time you're heading into the water to rescue yet another struggling swimmer, look over your shoulder. You'll notice that the people you've pulled up onto the beach have an annoying habit.

They keep getting *back* into the water.

You'd think someone who's just been rescued and retched out a

lungful of brackish saltwater would have the sense to sit where it's
safe. But you'd be wrong.

Somehow, they didn't get the message that the water is dangerous
for the ill-prepared. They go merrily back to what they were doing
until once again a leg cramp or the cold or panic or simple weariness
requires that you once again swim out to rescue them.

What is *wrong* with these people?

Bored on the beach

After you've splashed around in the water, sitting on the beach
can be…boring. There's nothing to do. It's hot. There's never an ice
cream vendor handy.

So before long it's just natural to pad across the wet sand and ease
back into the water. And what could possibly go wrong with cooling
off your toes? People tell themselves that they've learned their lessons; they'll just do a bit of wading—up to their knees, max—and
then call it a day. Well, up to their waists, but that's nothing. Okay,
maybe it makes sense to get out a bit deeper—no sense in sunburning
the old shoulders.

The fundamental problem isn't with the rescued people. They're
just being people. People are inclined to return to past behavior unless they're taught to do otherwise. It's our nature to repeat mistakes
unless someone helps us see alternatives.

The problem is with us lifeguards. *We're* in charge of the beach,
and we're doing nothing to teach rescued people the dangers of going
back out into the water.

If evangelism is pulling people to safety, then discipleship is that
process of teaching rescued people how to thrive on the beach.

Evangelism is great—and between classes, church initiatives, and
para-church mission organizations we've pretty well got evangelism
pinned down. We know what it is, how to do it, and what it accom-

plishes. The church, for the most part, is very good at catching the lost.

Where we're not so good is hanging onto the newly-converted.

Listen: thank God we've got lifeguards around. I'm one of the people who was spiritually rescued and carried up on the beach. I appreciate those pros in Speedos. But it's time we saw that rescuing sinners is just part of the process.

We've got to do something that encourages the recently rescued to stay rescued. And that something is discipleship—teaching them to love Jesus.

I was sitting in a small café in the Philippines a while back talking with a man who pastored one of the largest and fastest growing churches in Manila. As we were discussing evangelism, he volunteered a stunning anecdote.

"Pastor Grant," he said, "we did a study of what happened to the converts after Billy Graham's Crusade in the Philippines. We found that about 80% walked away from Christ and that many of those became Mormons, Jehovah's Witnesses, or a member of a popular spiritualist cult that we have in the Philippines."

I wasn't surprised at this pastor's comments, but I was shocked when he told me why so many of those new converts became members of cults.

He said simply, "They have one-on-one discipleship materials."

I've been a part of three revivals in my life—the Jesus Movement (that occurred in America in the late 60's and early 70's) and also a revival in Russia after the fall of Communism. In both revivals about 50% of those that I shared the Gospel with became Christians.

In America it's estimated that 10 to 12 million youth became Christians during the Jesus Movement. In Russia, the statistics are similar—millions of Russians professed faith in Jesus.

And in both America and Russia many who professed faith later walked away.

I've been to St. Petersburg, Russia, twenty times since the early 90's. When the doors opened for Christianity, American evangelists quickly—and not so quietly—descended on St. Petersburg. There were hundreds of revival meetings with hundreds of thousands of Russians responding by professing Jesus. Today in St. Petersburg you'll find about 250 churches in that city of five million.

Three or four of those churches have over a thousand who attend on an average Sunday. The rest are congregations of twenty to forty souls.

I'm currently part of a third revival—one that's energizing Cuba—and it remains to be seen if we've learned to connect discipleship with evangelism. The current "walk-away" rate in Cuba is about 80% of new converts.

Eight out of ten new converts soon fall back into faithless living. That's a high price to pay.

But in one church—one that's actively using the principles of *First Steps* —they're hanging onto nearly 95% of new believers.

Prison lifeguards

Nothing illustrates the difference between evangelism and discipleship as well as what recently happened at Marion Prison in Marion, Ohio.

A few years ago Promise Keepers did a four-hour crusade at Marion—and they pulled out all the stops. Big rally, great band, first-rate production. Not only were the inmates at Marion invited, but so were thousands of other prisoners who could tune into the simulcast being beamed to more than 150 additional prisons.

The crusade was a huge evangelistic success—1,600 prisoners attended, and nearly 400 made a faith commitment to Jesus. A lot of men were pulled out of the water and rescued at that crusade.

And yet, the following week, there wasn't a noticeable increase in attendance at any of the small groups or chapel services. It was as if the crusade had never happened.

Think about that: 400 new converts, no increased attendance at Christian Bible studies or prayer groups. The new Christians who were *literally a captive audience* weren't showing up for beach events.

A man from our church attended the rally — as a *visitor,* he'd appreciate me mentioning — and he asked the warden what she planned to do with those hundreds of new believers. Though she was a Christian herself, she wasn't sure. Was there something else she *should* be doing?

My friend told her about our discipling program, and the warden invited us to come meet with her. We explained how *First Steps* works, and got a green light. She then introduced us to some men who became the first Marion inmates we discipled.

That was a few years ago.

At this point in my story, you're expecting me to tell you how God smoothed the way for a discipling outbreak; that now prisoners joyfully serve their sentences and sing kum-by-yah at morning count.

Not quite.

The program *did* take root quickly, and soon every empty room was reserved for one-on-one discipleship meetings in the evenings. Prisoners were emerging as leaders, and good stuff was happening. There were even men from outside the prison system coming in weekly to be discipled by prisoners!

One of the key leaders inside the facility was a man we'll call William. William was an independent contractor hired by the Department of Corrections to run the Prison News Network. Think of PNN as the in-house video shop — William and his prisoner team created video productions and graphics. It was both a training opportunity for prisoners and a support team for prison communications.

William saw the obvious spiritual growth among prisoners, so he decided to let prisoners take part in a baptism service. And while that may make perfect sense from a Biblical point of view, it's a *huge* breach of security in the prison world.

William was fired, and all the prisoners involved in the discipling leadership were first put in solitary confinement and then transferred out to other prisons. Standard procedure.

In one swoop, the head was lopped off the entire discipleship program. All the leadership was gone—and to make things worse, the sympathetic warden left for another prison.

Word got back to us that two years of work had been instantly dismantled. The leadership was gone, the program had a black eye, and we had a new prison administration to win over to the discipleship cause.

A quick call and we had a meeting with the new warden, who raised a hand to stop us before we could launch into an explanation as to why the discipleship program should be reinstated. She *wanted* the discipleship program in her prison, she said. Of the 60-some religious programs on site, *First Steps* was having the greatest impact.

So it was time to start over, right?

O, ye of little faith.

Here's what we discovered: *there were still 45 one-on-one discipleship relationships in place.* And had we waited a little longer, there would be even more than that as prisoners were not only discipled, but became disciplers themselves.

Evangelism is taking the good news to a prison and proclaiming it. Too often it's a one-shot message.

Discipleship is owning that good news and deciding not only to live it but also to show others how to live it too. It's a relational ripple that spreads and gains power as it goes.

You'll remember when Paul was under arrest he used the opportunity to share the Gospel. Well, what do you think happened when a guard accepted Jesus? Did Paul quit talking to him?

I wasn't there, but as a guy who understood the power of discipleship, I've got to believe that Paul encouraged new believers in the Roman army to grow spiritually and share the message.

Let me be clear: I appreciate the ministry of Promise Keepers in sharing the Gospel at Marion. It's *huge*. Nearly 400 men who were drowning in sin were pulled to the shore and given new life.

But the Promise Keepers organization would be the first to agree with me that discipling new believers needs to happen, too.

Take note: If you launch a *First Steps* program in your church, you can count on it taking on a life of its own. And it should!

For example, I just received a letter from a prisoner who was discipled at a prison where they're using *First Steps*. He was transferred to a different prison and has become the chaplain's assistant. He now wants to start a discipleship ministry in that prison.

And that's part of the power in discipleship: it reproduces itself. Once someone has been trained to disciple others and experienced discipleship, it spreads. And it doesn't take an event in a stadium to make it happen.

Which leads to the obvious question:

If discipleship is a biblical mandate (Matthew 28:18-20) and has such power in the life of a Christ-follower, why isn't more discipleship happening?

A good question. A *great* question. A great question worth answering for yourself...

 ## SINK OR SWIM QUESTIONS

- *In what ways do you think evangelism and discipleship are the same? Are different?*

- *If discipleship is a biblical mandate (Matthew 28:18-20) and has such power in the life of a Christ-follower, why isn't there more discipleship happening?*

- *In your church?*
- *In your own life?*

Prayer

Dear God, it's clearly your intent that people know you—and know you deeply, that they enter into a growing relationship with you. Please give us courage to share your story with others and patience to be certain those who come to know you are planted where they'll grow in you.   Amen.

4

~~~~

Clearing The Roadblocks

*Where we consider the two reasons many people
(and churches) never disciple new believers — and what
they can do to overcome those obstacles*

Imagine you're on a sight-seeing trip in the canyons of Colorado. As you're driving, admiring the tall, rocky cliffs stretching up on either side of the narrow road, you're praising God for his creativity and power.

Suddenly, you see several huge boulders in the road in front of you. They've broken off from the cliffs above and are blocking your way.

You quickly check to see there's no car flattened beneath the boulders, and while you're at it you put one foot on the rocks to see if you can shove them off the road. Nothing—they're not only planted on the road, but they've broken through the asphalt.

Unless you happen to have a bulldozer in the glove compartment, you're not going to be going farther in the canyon. But you were sight-seeing, so after snapping a few pictures of the road-blocking boulders, you carefully turn your car around and head back the direction you were traveling.

Now imagine you're driving the same road, in the same car, but with one very important difference: your child is lying in the back seat, pale and breathing with great difficulty.

Up ahead in the next town there's a hospital with a fully-equipped emergency room that can help your child.

You round a corner and there, blocking the road, are the same boulders.

What do you do?

Here's what you *don't* do: you don't take a few photos and turn around. You don't give up; there's too much at stake.

You'd be out of your car in a flash, carrying your child over or around the roadblock boulders. You'd hurry up the road as fast as you could and flag down the next car, truck, or rickshaw you saw coming your way. You'd give everything you had in your wallet and promise a kidney if that driver would turn around and take you to the hospital.

That's what you do for your kids. That's what you do when it really matters. You find a way through, around, or over roadblocks.

Two roadblocks between you and discipleship

Maybe you're past these particular roadblocks, but my experience is that most people aren't. They're stuck—and they haven't decided to move past them.

Most Christians who don't disciple others cite two reasons:

1. They're not certain exactly what to do—and don't want to make a mistake.

2. Discipling someone sounds like a big commitment—and they aren't sure they can follow through with that commitment.

I can appreciate the desire not to want to do a poor job discipling another person. As I've shared, I managed to do a *terrible* job when I first became a pastor. That's why so many of the sheep in my care wandered off, never to be seen again, at least in my ministry.

But the desire to take seriously the task is no excuse not to do the task at all. Performing surgery is demanding, too, but I'm glad some people have been motivated to master it. Putting out fires is difficult, but when my house caught fire recently, I'm glad some people who'd mastered fire-fighting skills showed up.

What's missing when people let fear keep them from discipling others is a clear understanding of what's at stake.

If you're following Jesus, you're not on a sight-seeing trip. You're driving through the canyon, and in your car's back seat are young believers who aren't able to care for themselves. They may not survive if you don't get them into a relationship with Jesus.

There's an urgency to discipleship. We may not *feel* that urgency, but it's real.

The urgency of discipleship

Look at how Jesus handled discipleship: when he was calling his twelve closest disciples, he didn't ask them to ponder his message or sign a petition indicating they agreed with him.

Jesus asked — insisted, actually — that they follow him. *Now.* There was *immediacy* in discipleship.

> As Jesus was walking beside the Sea of Galilee, he saw two brothers, Simon called Peter and his brother Andrew. They were casting a net into the lake, for they were fishermen. "Come, follow me," Jesus said, "and I will make you fishers of men." At once they left their nets and followed him.
>
> Going on from there, he saw two other brothers, James son of Zebedee and his brother John. They were in a boat with their father Zebedee, preparing their nets. Jesus called them, and immediately they left the boat and their father and followed him. —Matthew 4:18-21

And when Jesus described discipleship he didn't sugar-coat it. His frank description of discipleship wasn't the stuff you'd expect to find on a recruitment poster.

> *When Jesus saw the crowd around him, he gave orders to cross to the other side of the lake. Then a teacher of the law came to him and said, "Teacher, I will follow you wherever you go."*
>
> *Jesus replied, "Foxes have holes and birds of the air have nests, but the Son of Man has no place to lay his head."*
>
> *Another disciple said to him, "Lord, first let me go and bury my father."*
>
> *But Jesus told him, "Follow me, and let the dead bury their own dead."* — Matthew 8:18-22

And Jesus was amazingly clear that it came down to this: follow him…or there was a price to pay. Is it tough to be a Christ-follower? Yes…but consider the cost of not being a disciple.

> *Jesus answered, "I am the way and the truth and the life. No one comes to the Father except through me. If you really knew me, you would know my Father as well. From now on, you do know him and have seen him."* — John 14:6-7

My point: Jesus thought identifying with him and going about discipling others was so important that his last words on earth were about just that.

> *He said to them: "It is not for you to know the times or dates the Father has set by his own authority. But you will receive power when the Holy Spirit comes on you; and you will be my witnesses in Jerusalem, and in all Judea and Samaria, and to the ends of the earth."*

After he said this, he was taken up before their very eyes,
and a cloud hid him from their sight. — Acts 1:7-8

You can decide to disciple others…or decide that discipling others isn't what you want to do. But here's what you *can't* do: you *can't* decide that discipleship isn't important.

It is.

It's urgent. And the urgency is growing the longer we let immature Christians muddle around without the firm foundation of discipleship.

No more excuses

Discipling someone *is* a big commitment — but you've made bigger ones. I've discovered that discipling someone can be done in one hour per week, ten to twelve weeks per year. Add up the hours, and in a given three month period you're probably more committed than that to a television show or soccer league.

The *First Steps* program overcomes both of the roadblocks I've mentioned above. There's simply no longer an excuse for you — or your church — not to disciple others.

Which is good news and bad news.

The good news: you can do it. And you can teach others to do it.

The bad news: you no longer have any excuse to avoid discipleship.

Let's tackle those roadblocks one at a time…

Roadblock number one: "I'd disciple someone, but I'm not sure what to do…and I don't want to do it poorly."

Fair enough. At first glance this seems like a completely reasonable concern. And it *would* be reasonable, if it were followed with an additional comment along the lines of "So now I'll find out what to do."

But we don't find out. We don't go gather the information we need. Instead, we stop, take pictures of the boulders in the road, and turn around.

A quick question: how have you learned to do other challenging things? Things that required a certain amount of risk and commitment? Somewhere along the line you learned to drive a car, which was risky and challenging. Maybe you learned to skate or ski — again, risky and challenging.

As for me, I learned to be a competitive swimmer. And trust me: that can be a challenge. A risky one.

Swimming lesson #4

You can't win races if you won't get into the pool.

Maybe that seems obvious, but there was a time I didn't fully grasp the truth of that statement.

When I first decided to swim competitively, I heard about a swim team I could join. I think I was seven at the time, a scrawny little kid who thought he was a pretty good swimmer. And I was, at least compared to my friends.

Keep in mind my goal wasn't to develop my physique or cardio-vascular health. Nope — I was in it for the trophies.

I could picture myself blazing through a race and being handed a trophy so huge it wouldn't fit in the car. So I asked my dad to drive me over to the pool where a swim club was having its first practice.

I can't remember why, but we arrived late. All the swimmers were already sitting in front of the coach, who'd started the practice. That meant I was going to have to make a grand arrival — late at the very first practice. Not a good start.

Plus, I couldn't help but notice that there were *big* kids on the team — kids who were at least nine or ten years old. No way could I compete with experience like that.

And to make matters worse, I didn't have the right swimming

trunks. The entire team was decked out in Speedos and I was wearing baggy trunks.

I was late…I was little…and I was dressed like a dork.

My response was to look at my dad and wimper, "I don't want to join the team anymore."

My father smiled at me, took my hand, and then walked me in… and I went. But what else could I do? It would have been more embarrassing to start crying and run out—which was *exactly* what I felt like doing.

I was embarrassed. I felt outmatched walking in. And I was willing to throw away my chance to do something I enjoyed and my shot at winning a trophy so I could avoid feeling awkward.

You don't win races if you won't get into the pool.

It's more than a slogan—it's the truth.

Nothing happens until you get in the water. If you're not willing to take chances, there's no way you'll ever earn that trophy.

Maybe you will do a less than stellar job the first time you disciple someone. You'll do better the second time. And you'll be trophy-worthy the third time around.

If you're willing to climb into the water, God will help you finish the race.

And here's roadblock number two: "Disciping someone sounds like a big commitment—a commitment I'm not sure I can make."

Actually, the person saying this is being wise, counting the cost before beginning a project. Jesus himself recommended taking this step….

> *Suppose one of you wants to build a tower. Will he not first sit down and estimate the cost to see if he has enough money to complete it? For if he lays the foundation and is not able to finish it, everyone who sees it will ridicule him,*

saying, "This fellow began to build and was not able to finish." — Luke 14:28-30

Note that Jesus' comments were made in the context of explaining what it costs to *be* his disciple. The same principle applies when it comes to determining what it takes to *do* discipling.

Most people think discipling another person is time-consuming and demanding, falling somewhere between being on call and inviting the person being discipled to live in your basement.

Relax — discipling another to love Jesus isn't a 24/7 job. Well, it is — but the Holy Spirit is the one on duty around the clock. *Your* job can be done — as I've said — in as little as one hour a week, in ten to twelve weeks. I know, because I've done it dozens of times.

When you think about "discipleship," you probably envision the model used by Jesus. He selected twelve disciples, and they were with him pretty much nonstop for several years. They traveled with Jesus, slept beside him, listened as he taught across the countryside. A second wave of disciples ("The Seventy") were also trained. And then there are the multitudes who heard parts and pieces of Jesus' teaching.

That's seventy or more primary discipling relationships in three years. Jesus *needed* to have his closest disciples with him constantly to accomplish the task at all.

Besides, the notion of setting up a communal discipling situation was normal at that time. At the highest level of study, scholars went to renowned teachers to become disciples — often taking part in daily discussions and activities. Prophets and master-teachers set up "schools" which were more than the daily study sessions we associate with schooling. The disciples and their teachers ate together, lived together, studied together.

Jesus wasn't a pioneer in the model of discipleship he adopted. Plato founded the Academy in Athens in about 387 B.C., and it stayed open for nearly nine centuries. Euclid was another teacher who at-tracted disciples. Ditto for Phaedo. The Greeks, at nearly any time during a thousand year period, had enough discipling schools to or-ganize a basketball league. Now *there* was a missed opportunity.

My point: Jesus' approach to discipleship was culturally appro-priate as well as effective. But it's the *importance* of discipleship that we need to emulate—not the *model.*

The *First Steps* program does *not* assume that you'll add 70 guest rooms to your house and move in disciples. Why? Because you don't *need* to—and besides, think of cooking for that crew.

In our culture, the most appropriate discipleship model is one-on-one teaching. In our experience it's also the most effective approach. And if you want to engage people in our culture, the discipleship training experience can't take more than an hour or two per week for ten to twelve weeks.

When confronted with the two obstacles I've mentioned, at Fel-lowship Christian Church in Springfield, Ohio, where I pastor, I simply say, "We'll train you to disciple someone else, and you don't need a ministerial degree to understand the basics of the Christian faith. Discipleship is a three month commitment. And, every year, I want you to spend three months discipling another to love Jesus."

An answer which sometimes raises both eyebrows and a few questions...

If it took Jesus three years of non-stop discipling to prepare his disciples, how can you do it in three months?

Keep in mind Jesus was discipling apostles who would take his word to the entire planet. We're discipling believers to be effective Christ-followers who love Jesus and then continue growing for a life-time. Slightly different level of discipling, there.

Why do other discipleship programs take so much longer than yours?

Easy: they include material that doesn't really help people love Jesus. I can't tell you how many discipleship programs and classes include topics like "Tithing" and "End Times." Important topics, yes—but not essential for new believers.

If you want a new Christian (or an old one who's not done much growing yet) to love and follow Jesus, *these* are the important topics to explore:
- Prayer
- Bible Study
- Fellowship
- Evangelism and Discipleship

That's it—period. Everything else—no matter how essential it seems—can wait until a new disciple has formed a relationship with Jesus. Once that relationship is solid and growing, the rest of what a Christ-follower needs to know will be a delight to learn.

What's the difference between "discipleship" and "mind control and manipulation"?

Hmmm…a *loaded* question—but a fair one.

A bit of history: in the early 1970's, right on the tail end of the Jesus Movement, Juan Carlos Ortiz came to America teaching discipleship. His warmth and humor helped him connect with thousands of people who heard him speak and read his books. And his message was right on target: he taught about the importance of a relational, one-on-one style of discipleship.

Unfortunately, the discipleship movement his teaching prompted began to spin in an unhealthy direction and soon deteriorated into a culture of control.

In the late 1970's, I visited a Christian community in upstate New York.

During a conversation with one of the brothers in the community, he mentioned that he was looking forward to buying a car — if he could get permission from his discipler to make the purchase.

Maybe the discipler knew the man's financial situation and that a car purchase wasn't appropriate. Maybe the discipler was a mechanic who knew enough to look under the hood.

But my sense was that it wasn't either of those situations. Rather, it was a matter of control.

As the discipleship movement grew, more and more often immature believers began dispensing absurd dictates to those they were discipling. What had been prayerful, caring advice sometimes became little more than dictatorial control.

Because of the negative publicity (and devastated lives), "discipleship" became a bad word. To make matters worse, several cult groups also promoted discipleship as a way of teaching their heresies.

That's why Christians today tend to use the less-charged "mentoring" when talking about the discipleship process. There's less baggage, fewer negative connotations.

"Discipleship" isn't a four letter word. It's a biblical concept that can — and is — handled in a way that honors God and brings about growth in a young Christian. But because of the dangers, the *First Steps* program has strict guidelines in place as to what's appropriate — and what's not. How long the discipleship relationship should last. What's appropriate to discuss — and what's not.

You can find a summary of those guidelines in the closing chapter of this book. When those boundaries are respected, we've found that nothing inappropriate or damaging happens.

Two roadblocks — obliterated

So here's the bottom line: there's no excuse for failing to disciple others. Discipleship is clearly important to Jesus. It's certainly part of God's purpose for bringing the world to him. And the two objections—that people don't know what to do and aren't certain they can make the commitment—are answered by the *First Steps* program.

As a pastor, now and then I get to point out the obvious, and I want to do so here: *your church must develop a passion and a plan for discipleship.* It is without question a part of God's plan for your growth and his glory in your community of faith.

It's either discipleship—or disobedience.

Choose obedience.

 ## SINK OR SWIM QUESTIONS

- *Which of the two obstacles mentioned feel most significant to you in your church? In your personal life? Why?*

- *What would God need to change to help you overcome those obstacles?*

Prayer

Dear God, I want to be obedient to you. So does my church. If discipleship matters so much to you, we want it to matter to us, too. So where do we go from here, God? Please speak clearly through the rest of this book to me, and confirm your plans through what happens in my church. I'm listening, God. I seek to obey you. Amen.

5

~~~~

Four Essential Discipling Disciplines

*The fundamentals of discipleship
that lead to loving Jesus.*

There's just one difference between a beginning swimmer and an excellent swimmer: how they execute the fundamentals.

Watch a beginner and you'll see plenty of action: there's a belly-whopping cannonball off the side of the pool followed by an impressive display of splashing. As the beginner slowly moves forward, it looks more like he's participating in a water fight than swimming a lap.

An *excellent* swimmer splits the water like a knife blade. The dive into the pool raises ripples, not waves. The strokes seem natural and effortless, and an experienced swimmer will finish two laps in the time it takes a beginner to struggle to the far end of the pool. Excellent swimmers look as comfortable in the water as on land — perhaps even more so.

It's important to note that the difference isn't a matter of dedication. Both beginners and seasoned swimmers are dedicated — they've both jumped into deep water. They're both committed to staying afloat.

But dedication takes you just so far. *Beginning* swimmers become good swimmers by practicing the fundamentals until those techniques are second nature. And *good* swimmers become *excellent* swimmers by taking those fundamentals to the next level through proper coaching.

For both beginners and veterans, it all comes down to one thing: executing the fundamentals.

So if you're new in the pool, here's good news: if you'll learn and execute the fundamentals well, you'll get better. Your lap time will drop. You'll feel more comfortable in the water. You'll see improvement.

Of course, that assumes you're practicing the *right* fundamentals.

Your speed won't improve much if you borrow fundamentals from basketball and worry as much about dribbling as you do breathing. Or if you decide that throwing a pick on the swimmer gaining on you in the next lane is a good idea.

But don't worry—it could be worse. Imagine how the basketball team would look trying to take the ball down court using a back stroke.

My point: fundamentals matter...but they've got to be the *right* fundamentals.

That's true in swimming—and it's true in discipleship.

The fundamentals of discipleship

New Christians must also understand and practice the fundamentals—the *right* fundamentals.

I've been amazed at what some church leaders think are "fundamentals" for developing an effective Christian life.

Do new believers really need to master the ins and outs of tithing, the nuances of baptism, or the correct view of the rapture? Is that what will get them settled into their new lives and planted in the faith?

When we saddle new believers with that kind of heady—though important—information, it's exactly like teaching new swimmers to do back flips off the high dive board before we teach them to dog-paddle. We're giving information they can't use. Even worse — if they try to use it, we'll watch a novice go flying off the high dive only to drown...not exactly the result we had hoped to achieve.

To become a good swimmer, you need to know three things: stroking, breathing, and kicking. Nail those three and you'll go fast and far with a minimum of effort.

Most beginning swimmers breathe by lifting their heads straight up instead of turning their heads to the side — a mistake. Lifting your head straight up may feel more comfortable, but it creates a mini-dam each time it happens.

Kicking can be tricky too. Getting an effective kick means learning just the right amount of bend to put in your knees. Too much and your feet will pound the water; too little and your legs become wooden boards with no flexibility.

And the single most important fundamental is the stroke: placing your hands correctly as they rotate around your head, coordinating the stroke with your breathing, and making sure your upper body stays positioned to knife the water.

There are other skills and techniques excellent swimmers know, but these three fundamentals are the Big Three: miss any of them along the way and effective swimming becomes more difficult. Maybe even impossible.

I'd contend there are basic fundamentals for new believers, too. I've observed this thousands of times in our church, and in churches around the globe. If a new believer becomes proficient in these fundamentals, those new Christians are positioned to grow quickly and to move along efficiently.

Miss any of these four and a new believer will flounder...perhaps drown.

Think of these as the Big Four. They're the disciplines that matter most.

A little later in this book we'll also discuss four principles that come into play, too. They're also essential.

But let's keep things simple. First we'll deal with the four foundational disciplines. Getting them established into the life of a new believer is absolutely critical.

The four foundational disciplines of the Christian faith

About thirty years ago, I learned to ask Christians four specific questions. If believers were willing to answer the questions honestly, I knew how they were doing spiritually.

Even better, I could predict whether they were going to be walking faithfully with the Lord in several years…or they'd wither up spiritually and blow away.

Here are the questions:

"How fulfilling is your prayer life?"

"What are you doing for Bible study?"

"In what ways are you involved in church?"

"Who have you won to the Lord lately?"

The answers to those four questions give a clear view of a believer's spiritual health. That was true thirty years ago, and it's true today.

You see, I'd observed that new Christians who were actively engaged in prayer, Bible study, fellowship, and witnessing stayed faithful. They grew in their faith. They found joy in their relationship with God.

I don't want to be overly simplistic. Those four foundational disciplines aren't magic. Setting aside a few minutes every day to pray, read Scripture, and mention God to a friend at work won't guarantee someone grows in the faith. And weekly church attendance won't guarantee a young believer will still be attending church in five years, either.

But when Christians try to grow in their faith *without* those four fundamentals, I can pretty much guarantee failure.

Those fundamentals—prayer, Bible study, fellowship, and witnessing—have *relational* implications. They're how we get to know God better. And when new believers come to know God well, they experience God and his love more fully. It's that first-hand experience that brings joy, peace, and motivation to keep growing. The experiential relationship becomes the reason disciples want to dig deeper and stand firm.

Relationship is the best possible foundation for our faith because love is a motivation that lasts.

People come to God for all sorts of reasons—a fear of Hell, the pressure of a well-meaning friend, strong felt needs that the church can meet—but those reasons don't translate to a long-lasting, growing faith.

Consider the Pharisees: they knew all *about* God. But the disciples spent time *with* Jesus. There was a remarkable difference in how those two groups lived out their faith.

The shortcoming in many discipleship programs is that what's taught is pretty much the denominational distinctives of the teaching organization. It's as much an initiation to the denomination as a faith foundation. Yes, you'll learn to be a Christian, but you'll have to look exactly like your discipler.

I have a friend who says, "If you teach a new Christian doctrine before he learns to love Jesus, you'll end up with a legalist."

Sort of explains some things in the church, doesn't it?

Let me summarize:

1. A new believer needs to build a *relationship with God* more than he needs to master lots of information. More than head knowledge, a new believer needs *heart* knowledge.

2. The four fundamentals of prayer, Bible study, fellowship, and

witnessing help new believers spend time with God and depend on him…which leads the believer to a deeper relationship with God.

3. The new believer's deepening relationship with God motivates
    the believer to grow in the faith and fuels a desire to continue
    practicing the four fundamentals. And practicing the four fun-
    damentals builds an even deeper relationship with God.

See how it works?

And trust me—it *does* work. Believers—new or otherwise—who
faithfully practice the four fundamentals find that they're growing in
their faith, enjoying living for God, and seeing new light shine into
their lives.

Which is *not* to say that practicing the four fundamentals somehow
gives believers an inside track with God.

Suppose for a moment you're back out in the Colorado Rockies
again—this time at the end of October. You're tucked snuggly into a
cabin, spending your vacation days hiking and fishing, and one afternoon you notice dark clouds gathering above the aspens. The tem-
perature is dropping fast.

You bank a fire in the fireplace, shutter the windows, and fall
asleep—warm and safe.

The next morning you awaken and wonder what time it is. The
cabin is dark—is it the middle of the night still? A quick peek at your
bedside alarm clock tells you that no, it's nearly 9:00am, long after
sunrise.

Then you remember: *the shutters. I closed them last night.*

You pull on your slippers and pad over to a window where you
throw open a shutter. Instantly, brilliant sunlight floods into the cabin.
The day is brighter than any other you've seen on the mountain: a
brilliant blue sky and sunlight reflected off a field of snow stretching
as far as the eye can see.

Did your opening the shutter create the light? Of course not—it was outside the cabin whether the shutter was open or closed. But when you opened the shutter, you allowed the light in.

That's how it is with the four fundamentals. Prayer, Bible study, fellowship, and witnessing don't create light or relationship, but they do allow it into the lives of those who practice those fundamental disciplines.

If you've been a Christian for longer than ten minutes, you probably aren't all that surprised that the four fundamental disciplines are healthy for your spiritual development. This isn't exactly a news flash.

But *knowing* what's healthy for you doesn't mean you do what's healthy for you. If that were true, nobody in America would be overweight and we'd all floss after every meal.

Let's spend a bit of time exploring the four fundamental disciplines and how they can become disciplines in the lives of new believers...and in our lives, too.

 **SINK OR SWIM QUESTIONS**

- Answer these four questions:

  How fulfilling is your prayer life?

  What are you doing for Bible study?

  In what ways are you involved in church?

  Who have you won to the Lord lately?

Prayer

Dear God, you know my answers to the questions above, but I want to talk with you about them anyway. I want to be able to honestly answer them in a way that pleases you, that demonstrates I'm first and foremost your servant. Convict me of any area in which I need to grow. Shine light in any dark corners. I want to be a faithful servant who hears "Well done" when the time comes.   Amen.

6

~~~~

The Essential Discipline of Prayer

*Where new disciples learn how
to pray – specifically.*

I'll admit it: as a young Christian, I got bored with praying. One reason was probably that I tried to pray late at night in bed. I usually started out with a yawn and then drifted off as I ran through my list of prayer concerns that had arisen during the day.

I'd wake up eight hours later and then close with an "amen." I'm pretty sure when Scripture admonished us to "pray without ceasing," the idea wasn't to take an eight-hour pause in the middle of each prayer.

I was viewing prayer the way many new Christians view prayer: as a mental exercise rather than actual communication with God. No wonder I got bored so fast. It was boring.

It reminded me of teaching swimming back when I worked for the city. Those portable pools we set up were small—just twenty by forty feet. When you were first learning to swim, the pool seemed huge, but once you started swimming laps, it quickly grew boring. You did the same thing in the same small space, again and again. You were swimming, but so what? You weren't *going* anywhere.

Swimming becomes fun when you get past the tiny pools. When you're out on a lake on water skis, or shooting a canoe through white water, or surfing the Pacific coast—*that's* when swimming is fun.

You've got to get past swimming boring lap after boring lap in a tiny space you've outgrown. Otherwise, you'll do what I did when I grew bored with prayer.

I quit.

I just couldn't see why I should take time to sit quietly in a chair, close my eyes, and utter words I wasn't sure were being heard by anyone but me. What was the point? God already knew everything, right? Prayer was busy-work of the very worst kind.

Yet Christians I respected kept telling me that I needed to pray. So I stuck with it sporadically, reciting my list of requests and thank-yous, feeling for all the world as if I were reading a book report to a distant teacher who had to be as bored as I was.

Finally I prayed, "God, this whole prayer thing is boring. Can you make it something that I *want* to do? Could you make me *enjoy* praying?"

A few days later I was driving to the local mall when I began thinking about one of my good friends from high school. I hadn't seen him for a long time, so I casually said, "God, it would be nice to run into this guy again. I'd like to tell him how you've changed my life."

I pulled into a parking spot at the mall, walked across the hot as-phalt, and pushed through the doors into the air-conditioning. And there I immediately found myself face to face with the exact friend I had just prayed about.

"Wow!" I thought, "Maybe God *is* listening…and maybe I can ask for things."

I mean, if I asked for the right things—like the chance to share the Gospel with someone—the possibilities were endless. And if God could immediately answer a prayer about seeing a friend, what might he do if I talked with him about my empty bank account, my uncertain future, and the question that loomed as the Big Unanswered Question in my world at that time: Who was I going to marry?

Think about the role of prayer in your own life when you were a new believer. Was it rich — or perfunctory? Was it done with an expectation that God would answer and do so in clear ways — or was it safe and non-specific?

And maybe I should ask the question another way: how's your prayer life *now*? No matter how long you've been in the Kingdom, there's probably room for you to grow...so let's not miss any opportunity for God to touch you. As you read about prayer in the life of new believers, be asking yourself and God this question, too: *What's in here for me?*

The asking side of prayer

In Scripture the word used most often for praying isn't "prayer." It's "ask." God expects us to ask him for things.

But why? The last thing most of us want is to be nagged by a constant avalanche of requests. Why would God value them?

When you ask God for something, you elevate God and humble yourself. By asking, we receive salvation, the indwelling gift of God's Spirit, and everything else of value in the Kingdom of God.

To God, asking isn't an interruption. It's an opportunity to bless you and help you understand his will for you.

The message of the Bible is ask, ask often, and ask repeatedly. Good thing, too, because the more we ask, the more we learn about prayer. I've found I can never out-ask God. He loves to hear our requests and then see us notice when he answers. That's one way he's glorified.

Jesus said, "Ask and it will be given to you; seek and you will find; knock and the door will be opened to you" (Luke 11:9). Then — getting to God's heart when hearing our requests — he said, "If you, then, though you are evil, know how to give good gifts to your children, how much more will your Father in heaven give good gifts to those who ask him!" (Matthew 7:11).

When I was a child, I was an expert when it came to asking my earthly father for things. I asked for all sorts of stuff—toys, a BB gun, a gas powered airplane, three bicycles (at different times; I wasn't an idiot), clothes, expensive shoes, money for camp, a motorized mini-bike, a motorcycle, a car, money to date, more expensive clothes, a college education, and help for purchasing a house. I was amazingly comprehensive and dedicated to my role as Family Asker.

Here's what's amazing: my dad said "yes" to *all* these requests—and many more.

Not that my father was a pushover. He said "no" more than once, but not for anything that was actually, honestly needed. He was a generous man, and he often gave me gifts simply because he loved me, and he wanted me to have fun. The motorcycle fits into that category.

When it came to asking, I learned that timing is everything. My father was a used car salesman, and I discovered it was smart to ask for items costing money *only* on days when he'd sold a car or two. When he came home without having landed a sale, I kept quiet. When he came in after selling three cars, I asked for the moon.

My father gave me whatever he could, and as a child it seemed that there were no limits. As a father myself, I can testify with some accuracy that even the most generous earthly father has very real limits: financial limits chief among them.

But even that doesn't stop us fathers, does it?

My younger daughter was recently visiting my older daughter in Chicago. I called my younger daughter on her cell phone and asked if she had one of my credit cards. "I never leave home without it," she said.

So I told her to take herself, her older sister, and her older sister's husband out to dinner with it.

A father loves to be generous and give good gifts to his children—even if it's a gift given from a distance.

Now, this is a good time to point out that "asking" goes two ways in most relationships. There are things I expect of my children. There are things God expects of us. Authentic relationships include give and take, and God's clear that in our relationship that he expects nothing less from us than…well, everything.

We're described by Paul as "slaves" (Romans 6:16) because that's what we are: saved from sin and purchased with a price. Which means it is well within the rights of our owner to ask whatever he will of us.

The idea of having a boss—even a kind one who wants what's best for us—is an easy concept for new Christians to grasp. But the idea of having *grace* in our lives—being saved by grace, having prayers answered by grace, being in a relationship with God through grace—is a tougher idea to grasp.

Perhaps that's why God is so giving with new believers. He's helping new Christians see him as who he really is: a loving Father.

Jesus said that we earthly fathers are "evil," which I take to mean we have limitations, flaws, and failures. I certainly fit that description. Yet when Jesus wants to explain how generous God is, he uses us earthly fathers as a starting point. We have limitations; God doesn't. Our generosity is tethered to what we can afford; God's generosity has no bounds.

I've memorized Romans 8:32: "He who did not spare his own Son, but gave him up for us all—how will he not also, along with him, graciously give us all things?"

I took Jesus' statement, "How much more will your heavenly Father give what is good to those who ask," as something of a challenge. I've tried to test his limits and thus far my heavenly Father keeps surprising me with his generosity. Since I've been a Christian, I've asked God for the following…

- Enough money to live on when I decided one year to give everything I earned to the Lord. (God tripled my income that year.)

- My wife to be healed of a suspicious lump in her breast. (When she went in to have a biopsy, the surgeon couldn't find the lump. More about that later.)

- For $100,000 in the next five days after learning that our ministry would have to empty all accounts for a down payment on a new building. (Someone handed my associate pastor a check for $100,000 that week.)

- At different times for $12,000, $36,000, $8,000, $21,000, $15,000 to finance mission's trips to train pastors in other countries on techniques of discipleship. (All were answered to the penny.)

I could go on and on since my prayer journal lists hundreds of answered prayers. But you get the point—God's generosity puts our earthly fathers' generosity to shame. And he has unlimited resources.

When it comes to prayer, asking isn't a burden or imposition on God. It's a signal that we're ready to receive what God has for us that fits within his will.

So why don't we ask?

And why don't we ask *specifically*?

Specificity—the art of being specific

I want to explain the principle that propelled prayer from being boring to exciting in my life. And I want to show you how the principle plays out in the other foundational disciplines, too: Bible study, fellowship, and witnessing. I'll talk more about prayer than the other foundations, but be assured the principle works in all four foundations.

Here's the principle in a nutshell: *be specific.*

Most of the public prayer you hear in church and at the dinner table is so general in nature that we wouldn't notice if God answered the prayer.

For instance, when you ask God to bless you, how will you know if he does? Can you really determine if today was more blessed than yesterday? Okay, maybe yesterday your car broke down and today it didn't, but maybe that difficulty was a blessing because you were able to share your faith with the tow truck driver who showed up to help you. How would you know?

New believers don't get excited by repeating requests like, "God, bless me today," or "Help me do well in school," or "Bless my finances." General requests, repeated in prayer, become boring. Also, God isn't glorified because we don't notice anything that he actually does.

With my earthly father I quickly learned to ask *specifically*. I'd ask for a specific brand of athletic shoe and a specific type of clothing. I would never have walked up to my father and said, "Bless me today." Rather, I asked, "Dad, can I have twenty bucks?" My needs were real to me and very specific, and I wanted to make sure Dad knew exactly what I wanted — especially in the months leading up to Christmas.

One of my favorite Christmas movies is the classic, *A Christmas Story*. A young boy named Ralphie wants a BB gun, and not just any gun. He wants a Red Ryder Single-Action Repeating BB gun.

Ralphie's Christmas request is very specific, but he can't convince his parents that he actually needs or deserves the BB gun. The challenge is especially problematic since Ralphie's mother is convinced he'll end up shooting out an eye. When Ralphie writes a theme at school on the subject, his teacher pencils back the same remark: "You'll shoot out your eye."

Even the department store Santa delivers the same message.

Ralphie's chances of getting the BB gun seem remote — and on Christmas morning he rips open package after package without finding his heart's desire: the Red Ryder Single-Action Repeating BB gun.

Then as Ralphie's family surveys the mountains of torn paper, Ralphie's dad asks if Ralphie has gotten everything he wanted. Ralphie's response registers his disappointment.

That's when the father points out one present that Ralphie missed in the excitement. It's the right size and shape, but having his hopes dashed before leaves Ralphie only cautiously hopeful.

Then off comes the paper and Ralphie holds the object of his longing: a Red Ryder Single-Action Repeating BB gun.

His wide eyes tell the story, as does his reverent and excited, "Wow!"

That's precisely the response you'll be able to give when you pray specifically. You'll be able to see God work—and know that he's active in the lives of his people.

As you teach new believers to pray, teach them to pray *specifically*. To ask for what their hearts really desire.

Specificity in prayer is so important I want to spend a bit of time there—it's a powerful piece of discipling another to love Jesus.

Specificity in prayer

God is a *big* fan of specificity in prayer. That is, of petitioning God for something very specific, very measurable, very observable.

Many new Christians start out praying for specific things. They're like little kids in a candy shop. Someone tells them that God answers prayer, and right away they want to try it. And because they haven't been in the Kingdom long enough to pull their punches, they ask for stuff. Lots of stuff. Lots of very *specific* stuff.

And I've noticed that God tends to answer prayers for new believers on a regular basis. It's as if he's *looking* for chances to give them what they need and desire. I think God has fun blessing his children—especially those who are new to the family. After all, he's a father who loves giving good gifts (Luke 11:5-13).

I've known people who've prayed about cars being sold, for relationships to be restored, and—once—for a particular pencil to show up. No kidding.

A while back, in an Ohio prison, an inmate noticed a pencil his discipler was using. It wasn't standard prison issue, but it wasn't contraband, either. It was just something an inmate couldn't easily get.

One night the inmate prayed, "God, what a neat pencil Sam has. I'd like to have one like it."

Quick. Simple. Specific.

The next day the discipler, who was also an inmate, walked up to the guy who'd prayed for the pencil. He held the pencil out and said, "Last night God told me to give you this pencil. I don't know why, but here it is."

When you have something like that happen, it makes an impression. Keep in mind this was *just a pencil*—not a kidney, not a miraculous healing, not raising someone from the dead—but it was an answered prayer.

And unless you're praying specifically, how will you ever know your prayer has been answered?

Once we've been around awhile, we tend to complicate prayer. We hear more mature Christians pray and assume that what they do must be right—so we emulate it.

We pray in a solemn voice. We back off being specific about small things so we can pray more globally about bigger things. Instead of being a little kid who's joyful in God, we become weighty prayer warriors who are lifting the burdens of the universe to our Heavenly Father.

In the process we lose our simplistic, trusting faith that God is truly listening and that he cares if we'd like a pencil upgrade.

A specificity example

Some Christians get uncomfortable when I talk about specificity in prayer. They don't want to bother God with petty concerns. He's busy running the universe, right? Why would he care about you losing your keys—again?

Listen: God has already sacrificed his son on a cross for you. You've already been about as much of a bother as you'll ever be. Now he's looking for a relationship with you, and he's *encouraging* you to ask things of him.

But he wants you to ask *specifically*.

Following is a quick example to illustrate the need for specificity.

Suppose you're having challenges with your children and you decide to consult with a therapist. If you walk in and present your issue as "I'm having challenges with my children," any competent therapist is going to dig a bit before suggesting a course of action. Your problem is simply too vague; the therapist has no idea what you're actually experiencing.

The quality of the help you receive will be directly related to how specific you're willing to be about your situation. That's how it works in a therapist's office—and that's how it works in prayer.

You *could* choose to remain vague—and if you do so your first appointment with your therapist may go something like this…

Client: Thanks for seeing me. By the way, I'm having challenges with my children.

Therapist: It's good to meet you, too. You know, clients don't usually jump into issues quite so fast at their first appointment.

Client: I'm not like most clients. I know what my problem is. I'm having challenges with my children and I'd like your help fixing the problem.

Therapist: Let's get a bit more background before we start fixing things. How many children do you have?

Client: Three, and I'm having challenges with all of them.

Therapist: I understand. Boys? Girls?

Client: Yes. And I'm having challenges with them.

Therapist: How old are your children?

Client: Old enough to give me challenges.

Therapist: What sort of challenges are you having?

Client: Challenging ones, mostly.

Therapist: How do those challenges look?

Client: Challenging. Can we get to the fixing it part now?

Therapist: Let me approach this another way. When you're experiencing challenges with your children, how does that feel?

Client: Um…challenging.

Therapist: Do the challenges you're experiencing involve fights or yelling?

Client: No…just challenges.

Therapist: But what sort of challenges? I'm not sure what you mean when you use that word. Can you describe an interaction?

Client: Sure. At the dinner table last night we sat down to eat and there I was in one chair, and my children were in other chairs…

Therapist: Uh, huh…

Client: And my spouse. My spouse was there, too. And some pork chops.

Therapist: And then what happened?

Client: Then my children challenged me. Right there in front of the pork chops. Now can you fix it?

LONG PAUSE

Therapist: By any chance are your children out in the waiting room? Maybe waiting for a session?

Client: No…why?

Therapist: Because if they're living with you *they'll* need counseling, too!

Not a terribly helpful session. "I have challenges with my children" isn't nearly specific enough.

In my case, I have three children—all mostly grown, all mostly wonderful. And all completely unique.

If I were having "challenges" with them, it wouldn't take me long to realize that what was a challenge with one child wasn't a challenge with the other two. I wouldn't really have "a" challenge—I'd have *multiple* challenges. If all three kids were in rebellion, it wouldn't be for the same reason.

If I'm taking prayer seriously, my prayer would move past "I have challenges with my children" to "I'm seeing a rebellious spirit in my children. Please help me see what's at the root of that spirit in each of them."

As God honors that prayer—it's specific, motivated by love, and certainly cooperating with his will in the lives of my children—I wouldn't be surprised if God gave me insight to help me become even *more* specific.

As I thought about my children, it would probably hit me there's a common denominator in each of these three relationships: me. So in addition to what I'm already praying I'd add, "I want to be a father who reflects your love and values. I repent of my own rebelliousness in my relationship with you, God. I repent of my self-centeredness in my relationship with Barbara, my wife. I want to model your fatherhood, God. Please give me open eyes to see ways I can improve."

Far more specific, and far more effective. God would then know what I need. *I* would then know what I need. And when God arranged to drop a brochure about a Christian fathering seminar in my inbox, I'd notice it.

Why won't we be specific?

What's sad is that specificity in prayer is often actively *avoided.*

We tend to pray, "God, your will be done in Cindy's life. Either heal the breast cancer or don't heal it; it's up to you. Help her cope well or don't; that's your decision. Have her go through with surgery and chemo, or not. And we'll give you all the glory, amen."

Can you be any less specific than that? I fail to see how.

We couch our prayers in language so vague that, were I God, I wouldn't know what you were asking of me. Do you want me to heal your friend, Cindy, or not? Do you believe I have the power to stun the doctors with a clean bill of health or not?

We think that by staying vague we acknowledge that it's God's will that should be done, not our will. That's wise. But God's a loving father; he wants to know our desires. It's okay to be specific with God.

I've come to understand there are at least two primary reasons for our lack of specificity in prayer...

1. *We're trained* **not** *to be specific*

When we first became Christians we prayed specifically. It's intuitive. But as we hung around church awhile, we started to pray the way other people prayed. We moved on to vague, general, lifeless prayers.

Not good.

When you disciple a young believer, you must *train* that person how to pray specifically. Trust me: what's intuitive will be gradually bleached out of a disciple's faith experience unless you cement it in with modeling and training.

And if you're discipling someone who's been a believer awhile — well, then teaching specificity is tougher than ever.

Stick around — I'll walk you through how to do that training in a few pages.

2. Specific prayer puts our faith on the line—and that's scary

The second reason some Christians shy away from specific prayer is that specificity puts us in an uncomfortable situation.

What if you ask God to remove Cindy's tumor and follow-up x-rays come back showing the tumor is still there—and growing? What will *that* do to your faith—or to the faith of a young believer you're discipling?

Here's the problem: we've bought into the notion that a miraculous "yes" from God equals proof he's there and involved. But if that's the case, then a "no" must prove he's *not* there or he *doesn't* care.

It's faulty thinking, but it's how many people view prayer.

A model of specific prayer

Remember that showdown between Elijah and the prophets of Baal up on Mount Carmel? Elijah goaded Baal's prophets into escalating from prayer to frantic prayer to self-mutilation by equating Baal's actions with proof of Baal's concern. Elijah said, "Hey—maybe your God isn't awake, or he's taken a trip and you need to get his attention. Pray louder."

I think Elijah played that card because he already knew what God was going to do. Think about it: Elijah was a prophet. He knew God's purposes in this situation. Elijah had no doubt about the outcome. For all we know, God walked him through the entire choreography before the event began.

What happened on Mount Carmel was a great victory for God. But it *wasn't* a model of how we should approach prayer. We do a disservice to new believers to imply that somehow they, too, should equate God's love with his showing up with fire and thunder.

Now consider the prayer of three men who found themselves arrested for—of all things—being faithful in prayer.

Shadrach, Meshach, and Abednego found themselves standing before a king, rightfully accused of praying to God rather than to the king. After being reminded that the king had the power to execute them in an amazingly painful way, the three men had this to say…

> *Shadrach, Meshach and Abednego replied to the king,*
> *"O Nebuchadnezzar, we do not need to defend ourselves be-*
> *fore you in this matter. If we are thrown into the blazing*
> *furnace, the God we serve is able to save us from it, and he*
> *will rescue us from your hand, O king. But even if he does*
> *not, we want you to know, O king, that we will not serve*
> *your gods or worship the image of gold you have set up."*
> —Daniel 3:16

Now, *this* is a model for prayer.

Clearly there's no death wish on the part of Shadrach, Meshach, and Abednego. They don't want to be martyrs…they're very interested in God saving them from being baked alive.

But God's actions aren't going to determine whether they think God is listening. They trust God—period. And Shadrach, Meshach, and Abednego see themselves as they truly are: God's servants with whom he can do whatever God wishes.

Let's pause for a moment. What if God had determined that letting the three men burn alive would have advanced his purposes more than rescuing his servants?

That's God's prerogative.

What if Cindy dies of cancer in spite of our prayers?

That's God's prerogative, too.

Yes, God wants to give good gifts to his children…but we're seldom reliable judges of what's truly best. God is concerned with redeeming the entire world, you know—we're not each at center stage with the world revolving around us. We may be tossed into a burning furnace so a king will be pierced with regret and repentance and choose to revoke an unjust law.

A hard lesson, I know…but an important one.

I bring it up because we don't have to be afraid of praying for a specific outcome and then not seeing that outcome happen. It's okay. It doesn't make God any less powerful, or real, or loving.

When Jesus asked, in the garden, for the cup of his suffering to be removed if there was another way for God to accomplish what needed to be accomplished, I suspect Jesus knew the answer. He had to die for our sins so we could be forgiven.

But still Jesus asked. Specifically.

When Paul found his ability to do mission work hindered by some unnamed "thorn in the flesh," he asked God to remove the problem. Three times. And three times he got "no" for an answer.

Rather than assume a "no" equaled a "I don't love you," Paul recognized that God's answer was in fact a loving one, that God's grace was sufficient for him—even with the "thorn" still firmly in place (Romans 12:7-10). When Paul was weak, that's when God's strength could shine through him.

Encourage people you're discipling to pray specifically—for several reasons…

• *There's joy in answered prayer*

God has allowed me to travel a fair amount, and it's not uncommon for me to bring back gifts for people I love. Not because it's Barbara's birthday, or John's anniversary, or for any specific reason. I give the gifts because I care about the people and I enjoy blessing them.

I think in a small way that's how God feels about us. Sometimes he gives us wonderful things just because he loves us. He enjoys the simple wonderment and joy we express.

And sometimes I'll be asked to bring back a particular item because you just can't find it anywhere but the Philippines, Cuba, or

Russia. No, I'm not a smuggler...but I *am* a shopper, and if you tell me you want specific item, I'll try to pick it up for you.

Note to editor: probably better remove that last line lest thousands of people tell me they want me to buy them stuff. Editor? Did you remove the line? Hello? Anyone there?

The payoff for me of fulfilling a request is the look in the eyes of people whose wishes are met. I can only imagine how God feels when he's able to see the same look not once or twice but countless times.

I'm amazed at how people respond to answered prayer. Usually it's a two-phase response.

First, eyes grow wide as people realize that prayer actually works. Someone *is* listening.

And second, eyes soften as it dawns on people that God must love them.

Kind of like Ralphie with that BB gun.

Those are lessons I want every young believer to discover...don't you? It won't happen unless those people are praying specifically and can see God respond to their prayers.

That's why in the *First Steps* program, we not only teach specific prayer, we coach people being discipled to keep prayer journals. In my experience that's the best possible way to notice what God is doing—and when.

• *There's peace in answered prayer*

There's another reason young Christians need to have a vibrant prayer life: it provides peace during trying times.

When you've just given your life to the Lord, it's often a time that ushers in stress. Everything shifts—how you think, what you do, what you say—and it's a time of huge change. Things that were okay yesterday now bring conviction. People ask what's changed in you, and you hardly know yourself.

It's fun and exciting—but there has to be a place to experience peace in the process, too.

As for me, I find peace in prayer.

When my mother was killed in a car wreck, I found peace in prayer. When my house burned down, I found peace in prayer. When the pressures of ministry had me questioning myself and everyone around me, I found peace and freedom in prayer.

And let's talk about specifics.

When I first became a believer, at once I felt the confusion and black cloud of addiction tugging at me. I knew exactly what it was because I'd encouraged it for so long with hallucinogenic drugs. But rather than give in, I prayed, "God, please cleanse me from this desire so I can serve you." And God delivered me. The desire went away— and stayed away. The confusion, paranoia, and despair that almost drove me to suicide disappeared—instantly.

And when my wife was told she had a lump that required a biopsy, we prayed for healing—and God graciously answered that prayer.

An x-ray had confirmed that Barbara had a tumor, and that's when my prayers for my wife—a common occurrence—began focusing on her healing. I didn't ask God to help her adjust to the idea of cancer or help her deal with her emotions. I prayed specifically that God would remove that tumor.

When Barbara went in for the biopsy, another x-ray was taken, and the tumor had disappeared. Not shifted, not shrunk; it was *gone*. The radiologist held up two x-rays—before and after shots. In the before picture there was a tumor, in the after picture there wasn't one.

I was late arriving at the hospital, and as I hurried down the hall toward Barbara's room, nurses kept meeting me with smiles and laughter. Something was clearly up, but I had no idea what.

Then Barbara walked out—fully clothed and smiling. "There won't be a biopsy," she said, "because the tumor is gone."

Both the surgeon and anesthesiologist who were to have been involved in Barbara's procedure are members of my church. They were all smiles, too, and together we celebrated God's goodness.

It was a *great* drive home.

Now, keep in mind that God would have been just as good and holy had Barbara's tumor not been removed without any medical explanation. That's who he is—good and holy. But what a boost to my faith that God granted us that blessing.

And what a blessing that I was able to ask him for it.

I've seen prayer release God's blessing into my life—and new believers need that same experience. God wants them to have the benefit of his generosity and to learn he's a loving, giving father.

When discipling another to love Jesus, it's important to encourage the discipline of prayer. And not just any prayer—specific prayer.

After all, God loves us specifically. We can talk to him the same way.

How to disciple someone to pray specifically

It's been said that a vibrant prayer life requires four things: a quiet place to pray, a daily time for prayer, a rested body, and an alert mind.

Those are great if you can get them, but here's what you *really* need: a 79-cent notebook and a pencil. Even better—get a *First Steps* prayer journal!

We often fire off our prayers heavenward and then completely forget what we asked of God. And *saying* you'll remember is unrealistic; there's too much going on in life to keep track of every conversation—even conversations with God.

But when you write down what you've asked, you can check back later. You can see what God's done and is doing. And by taking a long view of what God's saying to you though your prayers, you can get a sense of where he's directing you.

For instance, if you consistently pray to go on a series of short-term mission projects and God's answer seems to be "no" on a regular basis—it might be wise to ask him what he's telling you.

When I'm discipling someone to pray specifically, I usually ask if there's an area of life in which my friend feels a need for prayer, if there's a concern he or she wants to take to God.

Then we work together to determine if the request can be made more specific. One approach is to sift the request through a series of "filters," of questions that usually lead to greater specificity.

Here are the filters that will lead the person you're discipling into more specificity…

Is the prayer obviously too general?

One way to determine if a prayer is too general is to ask, "How would you know if God answered this prayer?" If there's no way to tell, the prayer is too general. For instance, if someone asks for "God's blessings," how will that person know if God did, indeed, pour them out? In truth, we've all already received God's blessings in the form of grace. What else are we expecting—specifically? *That's* what to pray for.

Is the prayer coming from anger or pride?

When the end result of a person's prayer is that someone else will feel the wrath of God, it's probably a prayer God won't honor. Even a specific prayer ("Oh Lord, smite thine enemies…specifically Eric.") that's motivated by anger or pride isn't going to line up with God's best for his people.

Is the prayer motivated by self-interest?

These are fairly easy to identify. Listen for any request involving winning the Lotto, for instance. Or the quick death of a relative so a large inheritance can be realized.

Is the prayer for something the person can't actually handle?

An example would be a brand-new Christian who wants to be on the Amazonian mission field within two months. The person may have a passport and a map, but is he truly ready to go do cross-cultural ministry? Probably not. His roots haven't sunk deep enough into God's Word and a relationship with God to handle the challenges he'll face. And without strong, deep roots he'll be like that seed Jesus described in Matthew 13—quickly sprouting and then withering.

Is this request consistent with God's Word?

Our goal as disciples is to want what God wants. If our requests and desires don't line up with what he's already clearly described as his values and desires, I can guarantee he won't honor that prayer.

Is this request wise?

Some requests brought to God simply don't make sense. I might decide that I want to take up skydiving—I always thought it'd be cool and I never got around to it—but anyone who's had back therapy is just asking for problems if he jumps out of a plane. It's an unwise thing to do. Does the favorable outcome of this person's prayer put him or her in an unwise place?

Is the prayer connected to the calling of the person praying?

If Dave works as a race car driver, I can see the validity of him asking God for $5,000 so he can buy the best set of tires possible. Those tires could save his life. If Andrea has demonstrated a musical talent that blesses the church, and she leads others in worship, I'm up for hearing that only a $5,000 guitar will do. Fine. I hope God provides it for her.

But if Jack's praying for a new Cadillac because…well, just *because*…I've got to wonder if that's self-interest speaking rather than his wanting to be a better employee at work or servant in the church.

Look at the heart behind prayers. Is there a connection to the person's current career or ministry?

Does this prayer indicate a willingness to be obedient?

It really *is* up to God whether to provide a new heart for a transplant or to arrange funding for a mission trip. Is the prayer offered to God reflecting a desire to do what God wants—no matter what God wants? To honor God as good even if what's requested isn't given?

Be specific—in every aspect of prayer

By the way, I'm aware that prayer isn't entirely made of requests. We come to God to praise him, too. And I'd suggest that our praise is more powerful if we make *that* specific, too.

Its one thing to say, "God—look at that sunset. You're really…you know…wow…great. Amen."

It's another to say, "God, as I look at the sunset I'm reminded of your creativity. You're creative and powerful even when no one is looking. Thank you for the spectacular colors you've spoken into being, for the laws of nature you've put in place, for the ability you give me to enjoy and praise you as I see this sunset. Amen."

And if you think specificity is significant in making requests and offering praise, consider *repentance*. When confessing our sins, there's no option but to be specific.

But all that comes later. As you disciple a new believer, focus first and foremost on specificity in making requests of God and in journaling both the prayers and God's response.

There's power there…and joy.

There's also an opportunity to do ministry—in the life of the person you're discipling. We expect people discipling others through the *First Steps* program to pray daily for the person being discipled. Its remarkable how often God impresses in a discipler what specific issues are bothering the people being discipled.

Because that's the other side of the specificity coin: when we pray specifically, God answers specifically.

SINK OR SWIM QUESTIONS

- *When you pray, what do you expect to have happen?*
- *How has God answered prayers you've offered during the past three months?*
- *If you're uncertain how he's answered your prayers, what might the benefits be if you kept a prayer journal?*

Prayer

Dear God, I want eyes that see what you're doing in and around me. I want to cooperate with your purposes. Teach me to pray specifically — and then to faithfully obey you when you make clear your will. You're a good God — no matter how you answer my prayers. Amen.

7

~~~~~

The Essential Discipline of Bible Study

*Where new disciples learn what
to read in Scripture — specifically.*

A friend of mine describes how, as a young believer, he launched into a Bible reading program…

"I started the Bible like I'd start any book: on page one. Genesis was actually pretty interesting, what with creation, Abraham, and Joseph.

Exodus made for some exciting reading, too, with Moses, the ten plagues, and the Israelites learning to follow God.

When I got to Leviticus I bogged down in all the sacrifices, throwing blood into the air, and cleansings. What was *that* stuff? But I kept plugging and got through Leviticus — somehow.

"And *then* I hit Numbers. That's where I surrendered."

Some Scripture passages are more meaningful to new Christians than other passages. While all Scripture is inspired by God and useful for teaching in righteousness (see 2 Timothy 3:16), *not* all passages are equally relevant to new believers.

For instance, would you rather a new believer read Numbers or Romans? Spend time with Jeremiah in the Old Testament or Jesus in the Gospels? Focus a few months reading Revelation or the Psalms?

The principle of specificity that proved so helpful in prayer also plays a part in Bible study. I'll show you how, but first let's define some terms.

Bible reading vs. Bible study

Let's say as you're settling into an airplane seat you notice the man sitting next to you is reading the Bible. Is he doing Bible study?

Not necessarily.

He may be reading the Bible as literature. Perhaps it's one of the "great books" he always wanted to read, and now that he's polished off *The Adventures of Huckleberry Finn* he's tackling the Bible. He's reading the words, but they're having no immediate, personal impact on him.

Or perhaps he's a believer and he's reading for enjoyment, just soaking in the story of how God's interacted with his people. There's no specific point to his reading—it's just good stuff and he's having fun reading.

Or maybe he *is* actually studying the Bible—digging deep to see what the Bible says about something relevant in his life. He wants to know because he wants to be a faithful follower of Jesus.

What sets Bible study aside from simply reading out of intellectual curiosity, or reading for enjoyment, is the conscious awareness *the Bible is God's Word — and requires a response from us.*

Reading a Bible is a good thing—but it doesn't necessarily mean much. That's why when you're discipling a new believer, it's important you train the person to not just read the Bible, but to study the Bible—to read the *right* passages and read those passages *deeply.*

Bible study = work

Something else that sets Bible reading apart from Bible study: studying the Bible takes work. And it often requires coaching.

New believers need help selecting which sections of the Bible to read first. They want help understanding what they read. For instance, that time Jesus said if your eye causes you to sin, you should gouge it out—was he *serious*?

Bible *reading* is like a day at the beach. You show up wearing cut-offs, and you're carrying a cooler, sun block, a folding chair, and a good novel. Throughout the day you'll wander down to the water and dive in to cool off. You'll swim a little, splash a little, pick up a few seashells. Who cares if you get better as a swimmer? That's not the point; you just want to have fun.

Bible *study* is a bit more like deciding you want to become a first-class swimmer. *Now* a trip to the beach requires different gear—and you can leave the folding chair at home.

There's nothing relaxing about time on the beach; you're running, working out to strengthen leg muscles. And time in the water is anything but relaxing; you're building stamina and honing a winning technique. The day is all about ending a stronger swimmer than you began.

Generally speaking, we tell new believers to read the Bible—not study it. We don't train them to memorize key passages. We don't give new believers an appreciation of how the Bible is organized, and why it matters. And small wonder: as a culture we're so thoroughly biblically ignorant that it's a tragedy.

How ignorant are we? Researcher George Barna, in *Growing True Disciples*, says the single most popular verse among American adults and teenagers (a group which includes many, many Christians) is the oft-quoted "God helps them who help themselves."[1]

Pithy, but this isn't a Bible passage. It's a maxim from Ben Franklin, and it appeared in *Poor Richard's Almanac* in 1757.[2]

And the philosophy it sums up runs *counter* to Bible teaching.

Unless new believers engage in Bible study, they don't benefit from the guidance the Bible provides. Unless they memorize key passages, they're less protected in times of temptation.

Three assumptions worth noting

Please note the assumptions inherent in what I've just shared about the discipline of Bible study.

1. *I'm assuming the Bible is authoritative*

    I'm assuming the Bible is God's Word, and therefore has authority in my life — and yours.

2. *I'm assuming the Bible is supernaturally powerful*

    I've memorized plenty. Phone numbers. Quotes. Addresses. My wife's birthday. Bible verses. And while those pieces of information are occasionally handy, none are supernaturally powerful except for the Bible verses.

    That's because I believe the verses I memorize are literally the Word of God, and God uses them to direct me and protect me from temptation.

    The first verse I memorized as a Christian was Romans 13:14, "But put on the Lord Jesus Christ, and make no provision for the flesh in regard to *its* lusts." (NASB). I'd been a Christian for five months, was still single, and was still a teenager. Given my life situation, verses don't get any more relevant.

    Shortly after I memorized that verse I was walking down a street when an attractive girl in a kerchief-sized dress rounded the corner. Just as lust kicked into gear, Romans 13:14 popped into my mind, "Put on...Jesus...and make no provision for the flesh in regard to *its* lusts" (NASB).

    I had just one verse memorized, and God used it to help me overcome a temptation. To this day, Romans 13:14 continues to be there, instantly there, when I'm tempted.

3. *I'm assuming that you should memorize passages*

    I know, I know — some people don't memorize easily. And memorizing Bible verses reminds others of sitting in Sunday school classes where memorizing a verse earned you a gold star.

But I don't care.

I'm not suggesting you memorize to impress others or to garner gold stars. I'm suggesting — *insisting*, if I can use so strong a word — that you memorize select passages so God can transform your mind.

And that you train people you're discipling to do the same.

I point out those three assumptions because not everyone — including some other Christians — believe as I believe. Which leads me to suspect they've not experienced what I've experienced.

Listen, I'm not here to debate theology. But I can tell you this: if a new Christian doesn't have a proper understanding of the role of Scripture, there will be consequences…and those consequences will hinder the new believer's growth.

When discipling a new believer, it is absolutely *essential* you address the role of Scripture in the disciple's life. And expect the issue to arise: according to a 2006 Gallup poll, the Bible is taking a beating out there. Roughly three out of ten Americans say they believe the Bible is the literal Word of God. That's a drop of 10% over the past 30 years, and the bottom isn't in sight.3

So begin at the beginning

In the *First Steps* program, we camp out awhile on the authority and purpose of God's Word. That's because we know if a new believer *doesn't* view the Bible as authoritative, there won't be much motivation to explore and learn the Bible. If the Bible is just another religious self-help book, why take it seriously?

In discipleship sessions we consider what the Bible claims about itself and lead people being discipled through a discussion as to why the Bible is reliable. We look at evidence. We consider alternatives.

We then study the blessings the Bible says will come from hearing and obeying God's Word. Those promises are clear throughout Scripture, and we get them clearly in focus.

Then we put it to the test. We invite God to use Scripture to convict and correct, to lead and prompt obedience.

Scripture never lets us down.

I got confirmation early when that girl rounded the corner. God had just one passage to use to convict me, and he used it. Good thing I'd been advised to memorize *relevant* Scripture. "Go thou and do likewise" wouldn't have been the passage best suited to my situation.

Which leads to an obvious question: what are the most appropriate passages for a disciple to memorize?

Life Issues and Life Verses

I've discovered that new Christians generally have a single sin issue — let's call it a "Life Issue" — that causes them to stumble early and often. It's not the same issue for each new Christian, but I can tell you with certainty that there's at least one in every new believer's life.

That Life Issue may be lust, gambling, alcoholism, anger, a lack of forgiveness — there's a long list of options.

For me the Life Issue was lust. Hey — I admit it. It's a guy thing, and I had plenty of practice being a sinful guy before becoming a believer. In addition to having the propensity for lust hard-wired into my head, our culture embraces lust as almost a virtue. We use it to sell everything from clothing to cars, and we're barraged with lust-inspiring images.

Over the course of my thirty years as a Christian, God has revealed to me four Life Issues, and I've memorized passages — Life Verses — that address each of those issues. I review my Life Verses on a regular basis.

Life Verses directly address my Life Issues. I memorize those passages and then daily recite those verses aloud. I put them on like armor.

I'm *not* suggesting that *only* one or two Life Issues will create problems for new Christians. New Christians are just like us older Christians: we're *incredibly* inventive in finding ways to sin. And we're tempted in lots of ways, not just one.

But for all of us, there are one or two issues that have taken particularly deep root in our lives. They're like weeds we pull in a garden that keep coming back again and again.

And because our Life Issues are places of vulnerability, they're precisely where our enemy attacks regularly. They're places we need to be on guard. And they're places that memorizing Scripture will help us.

But not just *any* Scripture…we need to memorize *specific* passages.

Would you rather new believers open up their Bibles and wander through, hoping to hit something relevant? Or would you prefer they read from front to back cover, trying to keep everything they read in mind until they need the information?

Or would you rather direct their attention to specific, relevant passages?

As for me and my church, give us specificity any day. We want to identify new believers' Life Issues and equip those believers to handle those very issues. To do otherwise is to give Satan an easy route by which to attack.

I experienced victory over a Life Issue almost by accident, having memorized Romans 13:14, being tempted, and then having the power of God's Word ready. I didn't know the power of having God's Word planted in my heart and head until it actually paid off.

Jesus knew that power, too. In Luke 4 we read about the temptation of Christ…

Jesus, full of the Holy Spirit, returned from the Jordan and was led by the Spirit in the desert, where for forty days he was tempted by the devil. He ate nothing during those days, and at the end of them he was hungry.

The devil said to him, "If you are the Son of God, tell this stone to become bread."

Jesus answered, "It is written: 'Man does not live on bread alone.'"

The devil led him up to a high place and showed him in an instant all the kingdoms of the world. And he said to him, "I will give you all their authority and splendor, for it has been given to me, and I can give it to anyone I want to. So if you worship me, it will all be yours."

Jesus answered, "It is written: 'Worship the Lord your God and serve him only.'"

The devil led him to Jerusalem and had him stand on the highest point of the temple. "If you are the Son of God," *he said, "throw yourself down from here. For it is written: 'He will command his angels concerning you to guard you carefully; they will lift you up in their hands, so that you will not strike your foot against a stone.'"*

Jesus answered, "It says: 'Do not put the Lord your God to the test.'"

When the devil had finished all this tempting, he left him until an opportune time. — Luke 4:1-13

Note there were three temptations, and Jesus countered each one by quoting Deuteronomy to the devil.

Specific issues addressed by specific verses.

When Jesus himself is modeling a strategy for dealing with temptation, you know you're onto something. It's worth mirroring that strategy in your own life.

Here's a list of passages I've memorized that address impure thoughts. They're my Life Verses relating to lust.

But put on the Lord Jesus Christ, and make no provision for the flesh in regard to its lusts. — Romans 13:14 (NASB)

Blessed are the pure in heart, for they shall see God. — Matthew 5:8 (NASB)

Therefore, putting aside all moral filthiness and all that remains of wickedness, in humility receive the word implanted, which is able to save your souls. — James 1:21 (NASB)

As obedient children, do not be conformed to the former lusts which were yours in your ignorance, but like the Holy One who called you, be holy yourselves also in all your behavior; because it is written, "YOU SHALL BE HOLY, FOR I AM HOLY. — 1 Peter 1:14-16 (NASB)

Let the words of my mouth and the meditation of my heart be acceptable in Thy sight, O LORD, my rock and my Redeemer. — Psalm 19:14 (NASB)

I review these passages every morning. Now that I travel all over the world and I'm far enough from home that I could indulge any fantasy without being caught, I've never stumbled.

Am I tempted? Yes. Have I ever seriously considered doing anything that would offend God or my wife? No...and I credit the power of God's Word in my life for my ability to say that.

The power of specificity in Bible study—behind bars

I was in a correctional institution, teaching the principle of specificity in Bible study, when a large inmate stood up and stared at me.

I'm talking a big guy here. A guy whose *muscles* had muscles. A guy who could have bent me in half without breaking a sweat. And as he stared at me, I was reminded that I was locked in a room with the guy, with no guards in sight.

"I have an anger problem," the inmate said flatly.

No kidding. He was a convicted murderer.

"This is the first time I've ever confessed I have an anger problem. And I'm going to memorize five verses on forgiveness and God's peace."

Whew.

Driving home, I got to thinking: can you imagine the reduction in the crime rate if all prisoners could identify their primary Life Issue and memorize specific verses addressing that issue?

Even better—what if we *all* did that?

The Word of God is powerful and active—able to deliver people and set them free. But new believers aren't likely to study and memorize every page of the Bible. It's up to *us* to steer them toward portions of Scripture that will best relate to their lives until they're able to make those decisions themselves.

All of which requires that we accurately identify the Life Issues of people we're discipling.

And how exactly can we do *that*?

Sorting out Life Issues

1 John 2:16 identifies three major sin categories: "For everything in the world—the cravings of sinful man, the lust of his eyes and the boasting of what he has and does—comes not from the Father but from the world."

One of those three areas tends to be the stumbling block in the path of every new believer. Again—it's not the *only* place that a new Christian may trip, but it's a predictable problem.

Let me quickly define for you some of the sins that fall under each category.

"Cravings of sinful man" include lustful thoughts, adultery, promiscuity, one-night stands, overeating, laziness, pornography, sexual addiction, and other addictions (alcohol or drugs, perhaps). Cravings are an appetite that never seems to be satisfied. In many ways it's not the person who's in charge; it's the craving.

"Lust of his eyes" includes materialism, anxiety, depression, financial problems, overspending, selfishness, greed, and failure to keep commitments. I've seen adults who seemed to be children—if they saw something, they wanted it—now. They didn't think about the consequences. We may laugh about shopaholics, but when whipping out the credit card leads to bankruptcy, lying, or self-dependence, it's a sin.

"The boasting of what he has and does" issues include a desire for fame, anger, abuse, control, gossip, discouragement, bitterness, selfish ambition, road rage, hatred, racism, fearfulness, insecurity, low self-esteem, unbelief, spiritual blindness, skepticism, and seeking the approval of others in unhealthy ways. We're talking about pride here, and pride absolutely gets in the way of our spiritual health.

"But wait," you might be thinking, "are those long lists really all *sins*? After all, being proud of oneself is a positive thing—we teach children to have healthy opinions of themselves. We encourage patriotism and that's pride in one's country. And if it weren't for materialism, the American economy would tank in a heartbeat."

True…but that doesn't change reality.

While it may be healthy to have a balanced view of oneself, one's accomplishments, and one's possessions, a lack of balance (not seeing things through God's eyes) leads to sin. Feeling good about yourself doesn't change the fact you're a sinner. Being grateful for a $70,000 car doesn't change the fact you're not really the owner of that vehicle—you're its steward. God owns it, and if you don't see things that way, you're in sin.

These three sin categories are the Biggies for young believers. And you don't have to trust me on this—check for yourself.

In fact, *check yourself.* Are any of these Big Three at work in your life? Are any of them temptations that just won't go away? That cause you feelings of guilt and condemnation?

Read the list again and jot down anything that feels familiar or brings conviction. But don't write your list in ink; God's going to work in you to remove those things from you!

Here's what feels familiar:

Now see which category of sin is represented most often. Do you have one identified? That's your primary Life Issue. Write it below:

It's important that you identify your primary Life Issue, because *not* dealing with it leaves you in sin—and greatly decreases your effectiveness as a discipler. You'll be asking each person you disciple to go through this exercise; to be an example you have to be willing as well.

Dealing with Life Issues

The goal of discipling another is to help that person love Jesus. Again: you aren't there as a counselor or spiritual advisor. You're giving a focused amount of time to helping a new believer to develop a relationship with Jesus and learn valuable spiritual disciplines. That's all.

But that's an amazing amount.

And the disciplines you teach are the tools a new believer needs to deal with his or her Life Issue — especially Bible study and memorizing key Scripture passages.

Let me suggest this: when mentioning Bible memorization, don't present it without explaining *why* it's important. It's not memorizing for the sake of memorizing or being able to win a Bible trivia contest.

It's planting God's Word where it's available to help you fight temptation.

Here's a word picture to share:

Let's say you live in a cabin deep in the Minnesota north woods. It's sturdy and secure, and the loggers who built it 75 years ago were clearly captivated by the view of the river nearby. They built an extremely large window in the front of the cabin. It's the only window in the one-room cabin.

It's wonderful to have the view, especially during the fall, but now that the logging equipment is long gone, bears have returned to the woods — and windows don't necessarily slow down bears.

Every spring as bears awaken from hibernation, they're especially hungry — and each year one particular bear comes calling.

You've come home more than one year to find the window broken and the cabin trashed by the bear as she looked for food.

This year you want to be ready. As spring draws near, you drive down to the city and fill your pickup with heavy wire, lumber, nails, and a roll of razor wire. Then you drive home, unload your pickup, and get to work.

You build a strong reinforced frame and cover it with the razor wire.

But where do you place the frame?

You could screw it to the back wall of the cabin, or nail it to the roof. But doesn't it make more sense to place it over the window, where the bear is likeliest to attack? It's possible the bear could scratch away until she eventually claws her way in through the side wall, but before that happens it's likelier she'll waddle off to find another source of food.

Your Life Issue is the window through which Satan breaks into your life. The Bible verses that you memorize that specifically address that issue block his way — and bring you freedom. They bring you life. That's why we call them Life Verses.

And that's why you memorize key Scripture passages.

Following are passages that address each of the three primary Life Issues. Don't just glance past them. You've identified a Life Issue a few paragraphs back. Now take the next step and see which Life Verses relate to your situation.

I'm going to ask you to memorize at least four of the passages and do what I do: recite them daily. See which verses speak to you most clearly — they're your Life Verses.

Ready? With a pencil in hand to circle the verses that are most meaningful, read away.

Cravings of sinful man

Psalm 19:14: *May the words of my mouth and the meditation of my heart be pleasing in your sight, O LORD, my Rock and my Redeemer.*

Matthew 5:8: *Blessed are the pure in heart, for they will see God.*

Romans 8:1: *Therefore, there is now no condemnation for those who are in Christ Jesus.*

Romans 12:1: *Therefore, I urge you, brothers, in view of God's mercy, to offer your bodies as living sacrifices, holy and pleasing to God — this is your spiritual act of worship.*

Romans 13:14: *Rather, clothe yourselves with the Lord Jesus Christ, and do not think about how to gratify the desires of the sinful nature.*

I Corinthians 10:13: *No temptation has seized you except what is common to man. And God is faithful; he will not let you be tempted beyond what you can bear. But when you are tempted, he will also provide a way out so that you can stand up under it.*

Galatians 5:1: *It is for freedom that Christ has set us free. Stand firm, then, and do not let yourselves be burdened again by a yoke of slavery.*

James 1:21: *Therefore, get rid of all moral filth and the evil that is so prevalent and humbly accept the word planted in you, which can save you.*

1 Peter 1:13-16: *Therefore, prepare your minds for action; be self-controlled; set your hope fully on the grace to be given you when Jesus Christ is revealed. As obedient children, do not conform to the evil desires you had when you lived in ignorance. But just as he who called you is holy, so be holy in all you do; for it is written: "Be holy, because I am holy."*

1 John 1:9: *If we confess our sins, he is faithful and just and will forgive us our sins and purify us from all unrighteousness.*

Lust of the eyes

Deuteronomy 23:21: *If you make a vow to the LORD your God, do not be slow to pay it, for the LORD your God will certainly demand it of you and you will be guilty of sin.*

Nehemiah 8:10: *Nehemiah said, "Go and enjoy choice food and sweet drinks, and send some to those who have nothing prepared. This day is sacred to our Lord. Do not grieve, for the joy of the LORD is your strength."*

Psalm 91:11: *For he will command his angels concerning you to guard you in all your ways.*

Colossians 3:15: *Let the peace of Christ rule in your hearts, since as members of one body you were called to peace. And be thankful.*

Matthew 6:34: *Therefore do not worry about tomorrow, for tomorrow will worry about itself. Each day has enough trouble of its own.*

1 Peter 5:6-7: *Humble yourselves, therefore, under God's mighty hand, that he may lift you up in due time. Cast all your anxiety on him because he cares for you.*

1 John 2:15: *Do not love the world or anything in the world. If anyone loves the world, the love of the Father is not in him.*

1 Timothy 6:6-7: *But godliness with contentment is great gain. For we brought nothing into the world, and we can take nothing out of it.*

2 Timothy 1:7: *For God did not give us a spirit of timidity, but a spirit of power, of love and of self-discipline.*

Romans 1:17: *For in the gospel a righteousness from God is revealed, a righteousness that is by faith from first to last, just as it is written: "The righteous will live by faith."*

The Boasting of what one has and does (pride)

Psalm 63:1: *O God, you are my God, earnestly I seek you; my soul thirsts for you, my body longs for you, in a dry and weary land where there is no water.*

Jeremiah 9:4-5: *Beware of your friends; do not trust your brothers. For every brother is a deceiver, and every friend a slanderer. Friend deceives friend, and no one speaks the truth. They have taught their tongues to lie; they weary themselves with sinning.*

Matthew 7:15-16: *Watch out for false prophets. They come to you in sheep's clothing, but inwardly they are ferocious wolves. By their fruit you will recognize them. Do people pick grapes from thornbushes, or figs from thistles?*

Romans 5:5: *And hope does not disappoint us, because God has poured out his love into our hearts by the Holy Spirit, whom he has given us.*

Romans 12:19: *Do not take revenge, my friends, but leave room for God's wrath, for it is written: "It is mine to avenge; I will repay," says the Lord.*

Ephesians 2:10: *For we are God's workmanship, created in Christ Jesus to do good works, which God prepared in advance for us to do.*

James 1:2-3: *Consider it pure joy, my brothers, whenever you face trials of many kinds, because you know that the testing of your faith develops perseverance.*

James 4:6: *But he gives us more grace. That is why Scripture says: "God opposes the proud but gives grace to the humble."*

1 Peter 4:7-9: *The end of all things is near. Therefore be clear minded and self-controlled so that you can pray. Above all, love each other deeply, because love covers over a multitude of sins. Offer hospitality to one another without grumbling.*

1 John 3:16: *This is how we know what love is: Jesus Christ laid down his life for us. And we ought to lay down our lives for our brothers.*

 ## SINK OR SWIM QUESTIONS

* *What is your primary Life Issue?*

* *Which three, four, or five passages speak most specifically to you? List them here – write them out.*

    •

    •

•

•

•

• *When will you memorize those Life Verses you've identified?*

Prayer

Dear God, when I think about discipling others, I'm suddenly aware of how much in my own life is still dark, still hidden, still sinful. Please deal with me so I can effectively help others... and so I can be more fully a servant of yours. You are holy and it's only through your grace I can be your child. Thank you for that grace—help me love you more.   Amen.

8

~~~~

The Essential Discipline of Fellowship

Where new disciples form healthy
relationships — specifically.

Ever watch lions hunt?
Even if your only safari experience was on the Nature Channel, an image probably comes to mind.

A female lion (they do most of the hunting, you know, though the male lions always eat first…*there's* a system worth further study) lies quietly in tall grass near a water hole. She's motionless. Only her eyes move as she studies a small herd of zebra approaching the muddy water to drink.

The herd is nervous, jittery, ready to bolt at the first sign of movement. Good thing, too, because somewhere in their collective memory is a nagging suspicion that Bad Things Have Happened Here Before.

As the herd grows more comfortable, the zebras break formation. A few zebras notice there's juicy grass over on the other side of the pond, so they wander over to graze. A couple of the younger zebras break out a Frisbee™ and start to toss it around. I don't actually pay a lot of attention to what zebras do when they decide to picnic; I'm too busy watching the lion…who's busy watching the zebras.

Sooner or later one lone zebra wanders a little too far from the rest of the herd.

And that's the precise moment two things happen.

The first is, if you're like me, that you start screaming at the television, "Turn around! Get back with the other guys! Don't you even see that lion?"

And the second thing that happens is that what looked like a brown rock explodes into action. The lioness is on that startled zebra in an instant, all teeth and claws, and it isn't pretty.

Apparently zebras don't watch a lot of cable television. If they did, they'd know that lions *always* go after the strays first. Zebras who hang out in the middle of the herd never even bother to buy life insurance — they're going to live forever.

But zebras who venture out on their own?

They're going to be lunch.

The hunt for new believers

I don't view Satan as a symbol of evil, or a theological sticky point. I view him as he's described in Scripture: as a tempter (Mark 1:13), as an enemy (Matthew 13:39), and as intentional in his desire to cause believers harm.

And remember Peter's description of Satan:

> *Your enemy the devil prowls around like a roaring lion looking for someone to devour. Resist him, standing firm in the faith, because you know that your brothers throughout the world are undergoing the same kind of sufferings.* —
> 1 Peter 5: 8-9

A lion — and a malicious one at that.

And who do lions find to be their easiest prey?

The strays.

The power of authentic fellowship

Satan absolutely wants new believers to attempt to go it alone. That's when they're most vulnerable to his attacks. Satan will manipulate and lie and deceive — anything to drive wedges between new believers and older, more mature believers.

Anything to alienate new believers from the church so they fall back into their old destructive friendships and patterns. Anything to weaken the ties of new believers with people who might disciple those new believers.

But why? Why is keeping new believers alone so important to Satan? It's because fellowship — authentic fellowship — is critical to the success of a new Christ follower.

And to the success of the church.

What *is* fellowship?

Some churches define "fellowship" as anything that gets church members together. Potlucks, Gospel sings, service projects, scrap booking, the church softball league — they're all fellowship.

They're all *relational*, true…but they aren't necessarily all "fellowship."

Fellowship defined

Defining "fellowship" is worth the effort because, unless a new believer is tied into the real deal, something will be missing. The encouragement and support new Christians desperately need will never quite materialize.

Which means a new believer will be a spiritual stray…and vulnerable.

Fellowship can happen in one of three relational groupings. Here's an easy way to remember them: picture three buildings sitting next to each other. But not just any buildings.

The first building is huge. It's a Stadium that holds thousands of cheering fans at a sporting event or a concert.

The second building is the size of a small house. It's the Stadium's Parking Administration Building. Here's where parking lot attendants hang out before those big events. In the building is a little meeting room that seats up to fifteen people.

The last building is over by the entrance to the Stadium. It's a Guard Shack and it's where parking lot attendants sit while taking your ten bucks. Two people can get in the shack, but they'd better be friendly: they'll be sitting close.

Got those three buildings in mind? They're...

1. The Stadium that holds large groups.
2. The Parking Administration Building where small groups meet.
3. The Guard Shack where only two people fit.

Jesus did ministry with people in all three of those groupings while he was here on earth. We do ministry in the same groupings today. If a new believer is going to experience fellowship, it has to happen in one of those three places.

Welcome to the Stadium

The stadium represents *large group* meetings. Jesus held them—he preached to multitudes on more than one occasion. A large group meeting is just what it sounds like—a big bunch of people gathered together.

Sunday morning church services tend to be large groups. You walk in, you sit down, and you're a face in the crowd. While there's something magnificent about being with hundreds or thousands of others as you're worshipping God, singing praises, and standing together in prayer, there's also a feeling of anonymity.

Large groups are tough places to form relationships.

First time visitors to mega-churches are often reminded of attending concerts or sporting events — that's the only other place these visitors have been in so large a crowd. It's understandable when they start looking around for cheerleaders.

Welcome to the Parking Administration Building

This building represents *small groups.* Jesus often met with small groups — his *disciples* were a small group. It's no stretch to imagine Jesus in the Parking Administration Building meeting room sitting with his disciples, feet up on the table, coffee cup in hand. Well, maybe the coffee cup is a stretch.

A new Christian is far more likely to form relationships in a small group than in a large group. Small groups are where we make connections, learn names, focus on faces, tell our stories.

Welcome to the Guard Shack.

Here's where relationships have the greatest potential to deepen most. Jesus was constantly singling out people and interacting with them. A short man who climbed a tree for a better view. A woman fetching water from a well. A blind man sitting by the curb.

One-on-one interaction is where relationships form fastest and grow strongest. Even in a small group there are usually one or two people we're drawn to most naturally. They become the people with whom we're comfortable sharing the Guard Shack.

There's nothing particularly spiritual about any of these three groupings of people. Large group, small group, one-on-one: it's how we do life. But it's not necessarily how we *find* life.

We find life — the fellowship we need and crave — when three relational qualities happen in the context of those groupings.

True fellowship happens when we experience faith, hope, and love. They're the heartbeat of authentic fellowship — and of healthy relationships. If we find them in a large group setting, that large group is fellowship. If we experience them in a small group — it's fellowship. If we experience faith, hope, and love in a one-on-one relationship with another believer, *that's* fellowship.

Fellowship is *not* just getting together with other Christians. If faith, hope, and love aren't there, our get-together is empty at best.

Faith is essentially a deep trust in God. There are people who encourage us in living faithfully, who know us transparently, and who honestly believe in us. Who inspire or instruct us to grow in our relationship with God. These are people with whom we can enjoy deep fellowship.

Hope is the positive realization we're all in this together, and as we move through life together, we'll see a light at the end of the tunnel. Without hope all we have is discouragement — not a great platform for victorious living. We all need the encouragement of hopeful people.

Love, as expressed in relationship, is often simply listening and then acting in another person's best interests. How love looks depends on what the other person needs — but it's always attentive, always forgiving, always desiring the best possible outcome.

Fellowship happens...or not

In many churches, a new Christian is asked to dive into regular church attendance, and that's encouraging, inspiring, and educational — but it's not fellowship. Meeting a hundred people with a handshake doesn't allow faith, hope, or love to develop.

If we can convince a new Christian to join a small group (or force the issue by making the new believer attend a New Members' Class), then there's a greater chance for relational connections to develop. But what sort of connections? There may be faith, hope, and love evidenced — but maybe not.

The best chance for faith, hope, and love to happen is in a one-on-one relationship. That's one reason we launch a new Christian into a discipleship relationship as soon as possible.

Disciplers model fellowship

A discipleship relationship models fellowship. Disciplers trust God and teach new believers to do the same. Disciplers are hopeful for the new believer's life in Christ. Disciplers are loving, expressing their love through a very visible commitment to disciple the new believer.

And there's a secret power in discipling: what's modeled makes a far longer-lasting impression than what's said. The Christian faith is caught more than taught. Disciplers show new believers what fellowship looks like.

But we don't consider a discipler's job finished until the person being discipled transitions into an appropriate small group, too. That's where additional healthy relationships can be formed and where fellowship can become a regular part of life.

Until a new Christian is regularly in fellowship, that new believer is a stray, wandering alone without adequate encouragement and protection. The enemy *will* seek to intercept and destroy that young Christian — guaranteed.

The benefits of discipleship

We tend to think that fellowship is all about us. That when we're in fellowship we're better able to withstand temptation and find it easier to worship God. That we'll experience more encouragement. And that's all true — those are very real benefits of fellowship.

But God doesn't want us to be in fellowship for those reasons *only.*

Authentic fellowship is a witness

Jesus was big on relationships, and not just so his twelve disciples would have someone to chat with as they hiked from town to town. Jesus urged his followers to be in relationships praying that "they be brought to complete unity to let the world know that you sent me" (John 17:23).

When Christians are in fellowship, walking in unity, the world witnesses the reality of Jesus.

Here's a tough truth for us preachers: we think our sermons motivate people to consider the Kingdom and come to Christ. And maybe we do have some impact.

But if you've got a healthy, interracial small group that meets regularly in a town where there's racial tension — *that's* impact.

If your church is full of people from all ages and economic backgrounds — *that's* impact.

If walking into your church is like walking into a family reunion where everyone is invited — *that's* impact.

Christians loving each other in godly, healthy, practical ways got attention in Jesus' time and they get attention now. Their lives are a testimony that simply can't be dismissed.

Fellowship often draws unchurched people to the church. And it's fellowship — connecting with others in authentic, healthy ways — that can keep them there.

Authentic fellowship plugs us into ministry

God assumed we'd be in fellowship, so he designed the church accordingly. He created the church so there were specific people with specific gifts that could be used in specific ministries. If a new believer fails to plug into a local church, there are others who are hurt as a result. At least one ministry will be limping along, not firing on all cylinders.

When we teach or model that active involvement in a church isn't necessary, we do new believers a tremendous disservice. New Christians — all Christians — *must* be involved in local churches to thrive.

I hear the objections being raised now. What if there's no healthy church nearby? Does a small group meeting in a living room count? And how about that guy on a deserted desert island who is totally isolated — am I saying that he can't grow in the faith?

To answer: any church that doesn't practice the fundamentals is ultimately going to be unhealthy, but near every Christian is *someone* with whom that believer can be in fellowship. That fellowship may happen in a sanctuary, a living room, or a booth at a restaurant where believers share a meal.

And that guy alone on the island? I figure his prayer life will be so good that he can handle no human fellowship awhile. And by the way, *there's* a guy who needs to pray specifically: "Lord, don't send a jetliner because it won't be able to land on this island. Send a *helicopter.*"

Church isn't an individual event. It's more like a relay race with each swimmer having a leg of the race to complete. The team doesn't win unless every athlete finishes the race.

Fellowship binds us together and turns us into a team.

When fellowship fails

Back when I was a competitive swimmer, I swam the backstroke on the medley relay. Medley relays are sort of relay potlucks. One swimmer does a lap with a backstroke, another does the butterfly, another does the breast stroke, and then the last guy in line does a crawl stroke. There's a little of everything.

The coach had me swimming the backstroke because that's the stroke I did best. I knew how to swim the other strokes, but in the relay I never did them. I specialized because that's where my strengths were.

All four guys who swam the medley relay race had their specialties. The butterfly guy didn't resent my backstroking, and I certainly didn't resent him (butterfly is very difficult stroke). We each knew our place and we worked together to win.

In Romans 12, 1 Corinthians 12, Ephesians 4, and 1 Peter 4, the Bible provides lists of specific spiritual gifts. There are lots of gifts mentioned, and even more plentiful than those lists are debates as to the exact nature of those gifts.

I don't feel any need to toss my interpretation into the pool to further muddy the water. And yes, you're welcome.

Here's what we Christians tend to *agree* on when it comes to gifts, talents, and abilities: they're all from God, and they're to be used to further the Kingdom of God.

One Christian can teach, another can make and give money. Some Christians encourage, others preach, some lead, and many have the gift of faith. Working together, Christians achieve victory. God has arranged the church so we *have* to work together to accomplish his purposes. We *have* to get along...sort of like four swimmers in a medley event.

One time my medley relay team was getting ready for an important meet. In the locker room we were psyching up because this was a *big* deal—a meet that would determine if we'd be going to the state finals or going home. It was all on the line.

Three of us suited up and joined the rest of the swim team to warm up. We kept looking for our fourth swimmer—the butterfly guy—and as our time to compete drew closer, panic set in. He was nowhere to be seen.

A quick search confirmed he wasn't in the stands, wasn't in the locker room, wasn't anywhere we searched.

The officials called our event and the three of us who were ready walked to the starting block—only to be disqualified because we were one swimmer short.

We later learned that, because he'd felt slighted by the coach for some reason, the butterfly guy simply hadn't shown up. He wasn't sick. He wasn't injured. He was *bitter*—and that bitterness cost us an entire year's work preparing for state competition.

I've got to confess: I'm *still* miffed about it.

Our missing butterfly guy wasn't bad news for our opponents, and they genuinely enjoyed our predicament. Since no other team lent us a butterfly swimmer, we walked back to the bench and sat down. The other teams swam their race, collected their medals, and a few stopped by to laugh at us.

It was *not* my best day...nor the best day of that missing butterfly guy.

I've seen a lot of highly talented, obviously gifted butterfly brothers and butterfly sisters grow angry and bitter. They leave their churches, often without ever explaining why. Or they may say plenty when they leave, slashing away with sharp words and pointed criticisms.

The church wins very few races when team members quit during the competition. Local congregations are left unable to complete the race God has set before them because there simply aren't the right people to do the job.

When you're working with a new believer, it is absolutely imperative that you help plant that person in fellowship *and* in a local church. When believers are alone, they're the least effective and most vulnerable. They begin to fall into two very real, very American traps.

The first is *individuality*. That value shows itself in the American culture everywhere—in broken relationships and even in who we Americans cheer for in the movies. We love watching someone beat the odds or the bad guys through determination and individual effort.

And a second plague infecting American culture is *bitterness*. It's swallowing us whole.

People can become bitter for many reasons. Sometimes there's been a deep hurt or humiliation. Other times there's unresolved anger that festers into something even more toxic. Bitter people close down, refusing to be in relationships. They refuse to trust. They become islands unto themselves—islands that broadcast "no trespassing" in signs ten feet high.

The good news is there's a Kingdom antidote for bitterness: forgiveness.

The bad news is that unless a believer is in fellowship with a brother or sister who has permission to speak the truth, the need for forgiveness is easy to ignore.

Fellowship is our best protection from the enemy without...and the enemy within. It keeps us from letting our individuality or bitterness separate us from others.

I know that happens because bitterness nearly took me out of the race.

The problem with my church...and me

About a year after I became a Christian, I was grumbling about the church I attended. I had a long litany of grievances: the older people who controlled the church were stuck in a worship mode tailor-made for seventy-somethings—and nobody else. Most of the church people seemed more concerned about money and careers than taking the Gospel to the lost.

And I wasn't too happy about the pews, either.

As I mulled over everything I saw that was broken, I began to believe that everything the church did was wrong. Fortunately, I still liked the pastor of that church and I listened to him.

I decided to give the pastor the benefit of my analysis, so one day I shared with him my lengthy list of the wrongs and offenses I'd experienced since coming to his church. The pastor listened, nodded, and when I finished he said, "You're bitter, and you'd better get over it."

I wasn't ready to lay aside my anger, so I challenged him. "Why is this *my* problem?" I asked. "And why do you think I'm bitter?"

"Because bitterness keeps lists, and you have a long list. Before long nobody else will be good enough for you. You'll be all alone, standing by yourself, too good for everyone else," he said.

That pastor then went on to say, "The mark of a mature Christian is the ability to receive God's grace and forgiveness and then extend that same grace and forgiveness to others. You're right that there are lots of things wrong with this church — and all churches — but you can't improve things by standing off to the side and judging everyone else."

That exchange taught me something I never forgot: every church has sinful people in it. Mature Christians receive God's forgiveness and then extend it to others.

That leaves absolutely no room for bitterness. And it requires that fellowship be characterized by unity.

People in our culture come together over many, many issues. Often it's about something they're against. If you think there's no cooperation in your neighborhood, just let the city announce that a highway by-pass will slice through your community. You'll be amazed at how quickly neighbors mobilize to fight city hall.

But unity? Deep, personal connection that involves truly knowing others, serving with them, and moving together with a common vision? That's rare — miraculous, even.

Even the gates of Hell can't stand against it.

Specificity in fellowship

Young believers need more than a vague notion that they're somehow connected with millions of other believers around the globe. They need to get connected with *specific* believers in a *specific* church. They need to struggle with offenses, and forgiveness, and being forgiven.

That's when they experience God's grace in new ways as it is granted to them…and as God's grace flows through them to forgive and bless others.

That's when they begin really valuing fellowship.

If you were to get that phone call you dread most, deep in the night, who would you call? It wouldn't be names pulled at random from your church directory. You'd call the people who love you — people with whom you've connected and laughed and prayed.

Specific people—and hopefully not just the pastor.

Look, I'm a pastor and I'll tell you straight up that I don't always visit members of my church who are in the hospital, or who are facing serious challenges. It's not that I don't care; it's that I'm not the best person for that job.

The best person is someone who's intimately connected with the hurting person. A discipler. A friend from small group. Someone who's in close fellowship, who knows what's really happening.

A discipleship relationship gives every new believer someone specific with whom to be in fellowship—the first, we hope, of many people.

 ## SINK OR SWIM QUESTIONS

- *With whom are you in authentic fellowship? That is, a relationship characterized by faith, hope, and love? List specific names below.*

- *In what ways do you intentionally move new believers into fellowship? What might happen if you accomplished that?*

- *Think about the benefits of the Stadium, Parking Administration Building, and Guard Shack. Which of these groupings are you experiencing fully in your church programming? What would happen if you intentionally moved more people toward one-on-one relationships characterized by faith, hope, and love?*

Prayer

Dear God, we lose so many strays to the enemy. So many of your newest children end up falling back into ways of living that don't honor you. We know it's your intent that no one should be without a relationship with you, that you want to redeem us all, to have us grow ever closer to you. Give us a heart and vision for fellowship that's more than having nice people hang out together. Give us a vision for fellowship that's powerful. Amen.

9

~~~~

The Essential Discipline of Evangelism

*Where new disciples learn to share
their faith — specifically*

When you're a competitive swimmer, you do without the perks other athletes take for granted.

Not that I'm bitter about it or anything.

Picture this: you're shuffling along with the crowd as you make your way into the stands at a high school football game. Hundreds — maybe thousands — of people squeeze into their seats. Down on the field a flock of cheerleaders whip fans into a frenzy as the home team explodes into sight.

A coin is flipped, both teams prepare for the kick-off, and you're on your feet, applauding wildly, your "get 'em!" lost in the roar. The band tucked into the stands blasts out a tune, but nobody can hear them as the ball arcs high into the night, sailing, then falling like a meteor.

It's first and ten, it's Friday, and it's football. Life is good.

For *those* athletes — those football players — it's easy to believe that, at least for one Friday night, they're the center of the universe.

That doesn't happen at swim meets.

Cheerleaders? Never.

Crowded stands? Well, if you don't count parents of swimmers, you could probably fit paying customers into a reasonably spacious phone booth. Sometimes the swimmers at our meets outnumbered the fans.

And then there's the ultimate benefit, the one most coveted by high school athletes: recognition.

After sinking a three-pointer at the buzzer to win the game, a basketball player can't wait for Monday morning. He (or she) knows there will be pats on the back, thumbs up by the bazillion, and everyone will want to say "congratulations."

After shaving a full three seconds off the school record in the butterfly event, a swimmer knows he (or she) will come to school and be greeted with…a yawn.

Competitive swimming is an invisible sport in most high schools. Nobody follows the events. Nobody attends the meets. When I was a swimmer, the only reason anyone knew I was swimming at all was the tell-tale wet hair in homeroom.

Actually, that's not true. Anyone who got to know me soon realized I was a swimmer because swimming isn't just a sport—it's a lifestyle.

The rhythm of swimming

Swimmers are the ones who can't party past midnight because they have to be in the water at 6:00 the next morning, getting in their laps. While their friends are chowing down on nachos, swimmers have to pass. Why? Because in the pool every extra ounce is like a boat anchor.

Swimmers discipline their bodies and adjust their schedules. They find themselves constantly explaining why they can't do something—or why they must do something—and the explanation is always the same: "I'm a swimmer."

It's not that swimmers *announce* they're swimmers—it's obvious to anyone watching. Swimming changes everything: activities, schedules, even a swimmer's appearance. There's a rhythm to swimming, one that's easy to see in the life of a serious swimmer.

The rhythm of evangelism

When someone becomes a Christian, there are changes that establish a new rhythm as well.

Activities change. Attitudes change. Schedules open up as "stay-out-all-night-getting-drunk" parties are cancelled and "be at church by 9:00" shows up each Sunday.

Friends and family members of new Christians notice something different. They see there's more peace and purpose in the eyes of new believers. There aren't cheerleaders on the sidelines announcing a conversion or a stadium full of fans applauding the decision; it's usually quiet.

But life-changes fueled by the power of God don't go unnoticed. They're visible to anyone watching. They're easy to see in the life of a new disciple.

And that's exactly why new believers are the best possible people to do evangelism.

New believers and evangelism

In many endeavors, the *last* person you want to represent your team is the New Guy.

Consider what happened to a friend of mine who found himself giving a tour of his new company—the day after he was hired.

"I worked for a publisher," my friend said, "and a couple times each week they had tours so visitors could see the place. Because leading tours was time-consuming and annoying, they gave the job to the last person hired in my department. You know, the person least likely to actually *know* anything.

"My second day I was handed a stack of index cards with talking points on them and a diagram of where to take the tour group. The idea was that at the first stopping point I'd rattle off what was on the first card and then move on.

"And that might have worked — if I hadn't dropped the cards."

The cards weren't numbered, so my friend wasn't aware that there was no longer any correlation between the stopping points and his monologues.

"It quickly became obvious that I was completely inept," my friend remembered. "Tour members were trading glances and just sort of gaping at me, wondering why the company hired idiots."

He got through that tour, but enough employees overheard him pointing to a copying machine while describing the giant presses in another building that he was never asked to lead a tour again. Ever.

"So I guess it sort of worked out for me," my friend added, philosophically.

New believers don't know much about the Second Coming or the finer points of tithing (net or gross? All through the church or does World Vision child support count?). They can't quote dozens of passages.

So why send them out to evangelize others?

Evangelism isn't a sales presentation

We've somehow developed a flawed idea of what constitutes evangelism. It isn't mastering a body of knowledge so all unbelievers can be argued into the Kingdom. It doesn't require an M. Div. or a black belt in apologetics.

If that were the case, no New Guys would be welcome. They wouldn't be ready — or effective.

But the New Testament model of evangelism is all *about* New Guys. It's Andrew running to get his brother so Simon Peter could meet Jesus, too. It's newly-minted Apostles sharing their faith with a dark world. It's people telling others their own stories of what Jesus has done—and that doesn't require a great deal of training.

What it requires is a story.

In our discipleship program we encourage new believers to do four things and to do them quickly:

1. *Deeply understand the Gospel and what has happened in their own lives*

   It's more than a formula or a process by which you join a church. The Gospel is a gut-wrenching, heart-healing story of love that's as personal as it is universal. Until a new believer truly *feels* the power of Jesus' story, it won't have an impact in that new believer's life.

2. *Embrace a "specific" method of evangelism*

   We encourage new Christians to ask God to give them a burden for specific unbelievers who need to know God—people God is already convicting.

   More often than not, those people are friends and family members of the new believers. And that makes sense—God now has someone to use *who already has a relationship with those lost people.*

   We disciple new believers to also develop relationships with lost people who are in their sphere of influence. Not to be inauthentic, but to be intentional and open to God's purposes.

3. *Master the basic tools needed to share the Gospel*

   By far the most important tool is the new believer's own story. We actually have new believers write out their testimonies so they see the story unfolding in front of them. What *was* your life like before Jesus came into it? Why *did* you become a Christian? How *is* your life different now that you know Jesus?

   Few—if any—of the more mature Christians in your church

could answer those questions quickly and coherently. They are absolutely unprepared to share their testimony should someone ask.

Don't believe me? Pick ten people in leadership and ask those questions.

We also teach new believers two powerful questions to ask others that open up spiritual conversations. The questions are respectful and open—the goal is never to "trap" someone into making a commitment to Christ. Those commitments—if you can call them that—don't last. You'll find those questions in our discipleship notebook.

Two additional tools: we have new believers memorize several key passages that make clear both the need for forgiveness and Jesus' willingness to provide it.

And finally, we teach new believers how to pray with an unbeliever to accept Jesus.

The fourth thing we teach is a reality check that helps start a discipleship process immediately.

4.   *Clarify commitments they hear*

It's important that when people make a commitment to Jesus they know precisely what they did, why they did it, and what they need to do next. And they're never more open to instruction than when they've just become Christians.

Notice that we don't disciple new Christians to recite a script. Or deliver a sermon. Those approaches are painfully inappropriate in the context of a relationship.

Instead, we help new believers think through how to tell their story and, in that context, tell Jesus' story as well. That's evangelism in its most potent form.

New Guys welcome — for several reasons

We disciple new believers to share their faith actively and intentionally not just because it's good for people who hear it. It's also good for the new believers themselves.

Here's why...

1. *Evangelism cooperates with God's purposes*

    There's nothing more fulfilling than seeing God use you in the lives of others. It's affirming, it provides tremendous purpose, and it's a shot of pure spiritual adrenaline.

    So imagine a new believer seeing God use him or her to impact the lives of loved ones. It's powerful.

2. *Evangelism cements new believers into their roles as Christ-followers*

    There's a common phenomenon that comes into play when someone makes a dramatic change in life — like becoming a Christian. In psychological circles it's called *Attribution Theory*, and let me explain how it fits here.

    Generally speaking, people want an explanation when they see things happen. It's just human. And a lot of great learning has come about as a result of that trait.

    Ancient sailors noticed that ships seemed to sink as those ships passed over the horizon: maybe the earth wasn't flat after all. Stuff dropped from high places fell and landed on low places every time it was tested; maybe gravity was a predictable force. A quick leap off a castle wall confirmed as much.

    We want to attribute things we see to a cause. We want life explainable in that sort of way — though it often isn't — and because of that propensity we're always trying to connect causes and effects.

    Got that concept in mind?

Now add this one: we also want to understand our *own* actions. Here's an example that came out of research done on, of all populations, blood donors.

If you've donated blood, you probably first did so because someone asked you to roll up your sleeve. A friend dragged you to a blood drive and because you didn't want to seem scared, or because you wanted to impress that friend, you gave blood.

But that doesn't mean you were necessarily willing to do it again.

Research indicates it isn't until around the sixth donation that people begin to *think* of themselves as blood donors. That is, they start to seek opportunities to donate regularly. They attribute to themselves the label "Blood Donor."

Now let's mix those two concepts and look at Frank, who recently became a Christian.

Let's say Frank was already a pretty stable guy—no wild partying or brushes with the law. But his work friends start to notice that when asked what he did on the weekend, his patterns have shifted. Sundays aren't devoted to yard work (or golf or fishing) any longer. Now he mentions going to church.

Those friends also notice that Frank's less volatile at the office—no yelling because a report is late or a deadline is missed. He's mellowed. Frank's friends want to know why the changes... and Frank tells them that it's because he's now a Christian.

The first time Frank says that out loud he'll be sweating. What if his friends reject him? What if they call him a hypocrite? What if they ask him to recite the 23rd Psalm?

The second time Frank explains the changes in his life by calling himself a Christian, it'll feel a bit more comfortable. Sooner or later, it will feel completely natural. He's attributing the label "Christian" to himself.

And his friends have a cause for the behavior they've observed:

Frank is a Christian.

Evangelism—intentionally telling your story and Christ's story—helps us associate with Jesus and become comfortable with that association. For a new believer, making that connection is critical. Evangelism helps cement that connection in place. The new believer thinks of himself or herself as a Christian and begins seeking opportunities to reinforce that identity.

3. *Evangelism builds dependence on God*

The first few times a new believer self-identifies with Jesus in public can be knee-knocking, teeth-chattering experiences. But it's those very moments that cause Christians to rely on God.

The good news is that evangelism always has this component. No matter how many times a believer strikes up a conversation with a nonbeliever and shares the Gospel story, there's always a need to rely on God.

4. *Evangelism inspires specific prayer*

We've already established that when a prayer is specific, it has tremendous impact. But I share that truth not just as someone who's done considerable praying,

I also share it as someone who has been prayed *for* a time or two…or twelve.

When I was in high school, I wasn't the least bit interested in God. I *was* interested in beer, drugs, and parties, which made Friday night *the* night of my week. Friday night was date night, drinking night, and party night. I wouldn't even consider taking a job that kept me busy on Friday nights. *Nothing* interfered with Friday night.

Nothing, of course, except my mother.

After I was ready for a date, I'd walk out of my room and head down the hall for the driveway. That took me on a path directly past my parents' bedroom.

Often the door would be open a crack, so I could hear a voice inside the room. It was my mother, and she was praying. She wasn't praying for world peace or financial prosperity.

She was praying for me.

For my safety. For my salvation.

My mother kept at it through the years, and in time her prayers were answered. I traded in Friday night beer worship for Sunday morning God worship. I traded in the drugs and partying for the ministry. I traded in the fun of Friday night for the joy of knowing Christ.

My mother prayed that I'd get to know Jesus because she knew a few things about evangelistic prayer that I've since discovered.

• *New Christians often report they were the subject of focused, specific prayer.* It's not uncommon for a new convert to tell me that someone who's been praying will be delighted with his or her decision.

• *Many new believers say "the time was right" to make a faith decision.* The clear implication is that there's a time that feels more conducive, when they're feeling more conviction. I'd suggest that intensity is a result of prayer.

• *New Christians often feel like a bunny wearing a target while half of heaven is hunting them.* Sermons they hear seem to be written with them in mind. Songs on the radio all appear to point them toward a faith decision. They run into an old friend who's now an enthusiastic believer. Or they turn on their televisions only to discover that for some reason the only station they can receive is a Christian station.

Don't laugh about God using television tuners for his own purposes, by the way. I heard that testimony from a new believer just this morning.

• *A sense of brokenness or extreme danger has shattered any illusion of invincibility.* An accident, a near death experience, a humbling incident, or the death of a loved one focuses their attention on mortality.

Lest you question my theology, note that I realize God is sovereign and dictates who, when, and why people become Christians. I'm not taking anything away from his awesome power when I suggest, though, that in my case, he had a partner: my mother. My Friday night fellow-partiers have not, by and large, become believers in the years since we got stoned and drunk together.

But none of the rest of them had my mom in their lives, either.

When I'd been a believer for several years, I did a little experiment. I began praying for people with whom I'd shared the Gospel by listing their names on a piece of paper and then reviewing the list several times a week. I noticed that people I'd included on the list were becoming Christians in greater numbers than the people with whom I'd shared but whose names weren't on my paper.

Coincidence? I decided to find out.

I designed a test to determine if evangelism—people making faith decisions—was somehow connected with specific prayer. I put 36 names on my list, prayed for all 36 people several times each week, and kept track of what I'd prayed. Two years later 33 of the people on my list had accepted Jesus as their Lord and Savior.

Okay, I see you science majors leaning forward and challenging the validity of my results. Were there other variables? Did I talk more often with people on my list than with people I'd not listed? Did I list only the people who were likeliest to make faith decisions?

The rest of you are wondering, "What about the control group? If listed people were coming to the Lord more often, why didn't you put *everyone* on your list?"

Look, I'm not a scientist. I don't design space shuttles and I'm afraid of lab rats. My scientific methodology won't impress any biology professor who's reading this. I know you can't quantify the results I experienced.

But this I *do* know: when you specifically pray for people to become believers, they tend to do so. Prayer and evangelism are somehow linked—and there's enough of a correlation I've committed myself to pray for specific nonbelievers.

 ## SINK OR SWIM QUESTIONS

- *What's your rhythm when it comes to evangelism? In what ways are you challenged or comfortable sharing your faith? How do you respond when you sense an opportunity for telling Jesus' story?*

- *For whose salvation will you pray this coming week?*

- *What would happen if every new Christian in your church was equipped to evangelize others?*

Prayer

Dear God, we want others to know you, too ... but we're often uncomfortable introducing you to them. Please give us a sense or urgency and purpose regarding evangelism. Help us share your story not out of obligation but joy. And though we're a little fearful to ask—please give us opportunities in the next few days. Amen.

10

~~~~

Three Months That Change Lives

*How and why three months is the ideal time frame
for discipling another to love Jesus.*

The first time I swam a complete mile I was eight years old. Swimming a mile was a stretch for me, but I was never in danger of drowning. Next to me in the lake, patiently rowing a boat as I wandered all over trying to find the one-mile buoy, was my coach—a very capable swimmer. Had I gotten into serious trouble, he'd have quickly pulled me to safety.

Thinking back, I wonder if perhaps he wasn't secretly wishing that I *would* start to sink. Then he could have dragged me into the boat and rowed home.

As it was, he stuck with me as I zig-zagged to victory. When at long last I touched the buoy, I glanced up to see if he was applauding.

Nope. Instead, he let out a slow sigh and nodded my general direction with a distinct lack of enthusiasm.

"Well, you made it," he said.

Not the words of a coach who thinks you're destined to set the world of competitive swimming on fire.

Disciplers and coaches

That coach who accompanied me on my first mile-long swim wasn't much of an encourager, but he did several things right.

1. *For starters, he was* **there.** No way was that coach coming out ahead financially. I've done some coaching myself, and even if you're tossed a few dollars to offset travel expenses, you're essentially a volunteer. Stop and calculate how much you're making per hour and you *know* you're a volunteer.

    The best coaches stay in the game because they love the sport—and love the players they're serving. The man who rowed along beside me on that lake was one of those caring, committed coaches. He showed up early in the morning and stayed late so we could get in a few extra laps. He drove us to meets and missed more than a few meals because he was at the pool, helping us become better swimmers.

2. *He helped me master the fundamentals.* Good coaches have an ability to move an athlete—even an eight-year-old one—along to the next level. They're able to see what the athlete needs to learn next and then drill in and teach that set of skills.

    The foundational skills put in place by that coach served me my entire competitive career.

3. *He protected me.* In swimming, like most sports, you can get hurt. Part of the coach's role was to keep an eye on storms rolling in from the north, to remember to hand out the sunblock, to help us avoid pushing ourselves too far, too fast.

    To the best of my memory, nobody on that coach's club was seriously injured the entire season. And trust me—that's not because the guys on the team were constantly careful.

4. *He had my best interests at heart.* The coach pushed me. At times I wanted him to quit and leave me alone, but along with the pushes came occasional "attaboys" that kept me going.

A good coach cares more about his players than his seasonal stats. And because of that he often posts more wins than losses.

5. ***And, finally, he was respectful and patient.*** I've heard horror stories about coaches who touch inappropriately or who fly into uncontrolled rages when a player makes a mistake. I'm sure that happens—but it didn't happen to me. My coach wasn't perfect, but he never crossed a line.

When explaining discipleship to people, it's sometimes tough to find a point of reference they understand. Is it a class? No. An internship? No, it's more than that. Well, is it coaching?

Actually, in lots of ways, coaching does sum up discipleship pretty well.

A good discipler *is* like a good coach. The discipler helps the person being discipled to master the fundamentals of the faith, protects the person, has their best interests at heart, is respectful and patient.

But there's a key difference: a coach focuses on something that's by definition fleeting. A discipler focuses on something that's eternal.

Think about it: no matter how spectacular a basketball player you become, eventually your career will be over. You may be all-state this year, all-pro in five years, and a hall-of-famer in twenty years, but here's the cold truth: in fifty years you'll be an old guy who can't make a hook shot. Your athletic prowess *will* deteriorate—guaranteed.

But a discipler who's encouraging someone to enter into a relationship with Jesus? Now *that* lasts forever—literally. You can be closer to Jesus in ten years, even more intimate in twenty, and eventually be with him in Heaven.

And here's another difference: a coaching relationship can last years. But in the *First Steps* program we limit discipleship relationships to three months.

That's right: three months...tops.

But they're three months that change lives.

Why three months?

When you're discipling a new believer, you'll find that person looks to you as an example of what it is to be a Christian. Fine—that's to be expected. But it can also be dangerous.

It's seductive having someone listen to you and then write down everything you say. To have someone consider you wise and spiritually mature look up to you. We don't often find ourselves in that position; there's a temptation to linger awhile to soak in the adoration.

And that's exactly the wrong thing to do.

In reality, our job as disciplers is to get the spotlight off us and onto Jesus. *That's* who needs to be known and loved. If a disciple enters into a loving relationship with Jesus, that new believer won't be disappointed.

But if that new believer decides that *we're* Jesus personified, and that emulating us is always the way to go, there's going to be a problem. We're going to disappoint.

A discipleship relationship is like any other relationship where one person has a great deal of influence and the other person has far less: it has great potential to become unhealthy. There can be an inappropriate dependency that forms. Pride can creep in.

We've found there are some commonsense rules that keep discipleship relationships healthy, and the first is this: *they last only three months*. The short duration of the discipleship effort keeps most problems from having time to form.

Besides, our experience is that the first three months following conversion is a critical window when discipleship has the greatest impact. I wouldn't say it's the only time a discipleship program is helpful, but I can tell you it's the best time. It's the time a new believer is most open.

And there's a pragmatic reason for three months, too: most people won't disciple others if the process takes longer. Nobody wants to sign up for an open-ended, seemingly-endless commitment.

The whole discipleship timing thing reminds me of a phenomenon found in nature — in some types of birds. It's called imprinting.

Imprinting — for better or worse

In the 19th century an amateur biologist named Douglas Spalding reported that domesticated chickens had a unique way of learning how to be chickens: after hatching, they focused onto whatever animal was closest and did what that animal did.[1]

The good news: when chicken eggs hatch, there are usually chickens sitting on those eggs. But should a young chicken happen to roll out of the nest and, peering around the barnyard, decide its mother was a *cow* — well, there would be a lot of therapy needed later.

Konrad Lorenz decided to test the concept. Working with incubator-hatched geese, he demonstrated two important details about imprinting.

First, the geese imprinted on the first reasonably consistent moving stimulus they saw. And second, that imprinting happened early — sometime within the first 36 hours of life.

Result: since the goslings had a bird's eye view of Lorenz's wading boots during the critical 36-hour window, they started following around the boots. Lorenz is often shown in photographs walking thoughtfully along, followed by a honking line of fuzzy little geese.[2]

Again: avian therapy will be required. But at least with a gaggle of geese, the group therapy rate will apply.

My point: new believers are looking for signals about how to live, what to believe, what's important. If that new believer sees a passion for God in you, that's where the imprinting will happen. If that passion happens to be expressed by a couple of Mormon missionaries who care enough to knock on the door with an offer of discipleship — *that's* where the imprinting will happen.

The first three months following conversion is *the* time to connect with young believers to get them grounded in the faith. Miss that window and there may be an uphill climb to reclaim lost ground.

Commonsense Guidelines for discipling another person

Following are eleven discipler guidelines and expectations we've found to be both reasonable—and necessary.

1. *Disciplers must set a good example*

Disciplers don't need to be perfect, but they *do* need to demonstrate holiness—to be living rightly before God. They need to have a heart for God and be authentic disciples themselves.

In 1 Corinthians 11:1 Paul writes, "Follow my example, as I follow the example of Christ." That passage sums up the heart of being a good example.

At our church we want disciplers to be known as honest and have relationships noted for integrity. They also need to be able to point to how the four Discipling Disciplines look in their own lives, to open their own Prayer Journals to share how God is answering their prayers.

Back in the '70's we called it walking the talk. Still a pretty good way to make the point.

2. *Disciplers must be ready to do the job*

To disciple another you need to have been discipled yourself. We require that all disciplers have gone through the *First Steps* program plus have taken additional training that prepares them to disciple others.

That additional training isn't theological in nature, by the way. It's essentially a chance to impart this list of guidelines and expectations.

The *real* preparation happens not in a class, but in prayer. A discipler must be in a healthy, growing relationship with Jesus to effectively introduce another person to Jesus. We regularly ask disciplers how *they're* doing, too.

3. *Disciplers must understand their role*

When you disciple a new believer, you don't become that person's boss or spiritual director. You don't control that person's life, dictate his decisions, or by proxy be Jesus in his life.

In fact, at our church a discipler doesn't even give directive advice without consulting a pastor or elder. To keep the three months profitable, there must be a steady, narrow focus on covering the material in the discipleship notebook and getting the new believer planted in spiritual disciplines that will bring life.

Disciplers are fellow-travelers, not the destination. They're shepherds who guide, not ranchers who corral new believers and slap a brand on them.

4. *Disciplers must be servant-hearted*

The best disciplers aren't in it to boost their egos. Rather, they have the best interests of people being discipled in mind.

Disciplers make available the time needed for meetings. For preparation. For prayer. And to do so willingly and with a servant's heart.

5. *Disciplers can't seek personal gain from the people they disciple*

That means no asking new believers to join a sales organization, or list their house with a certain realtor. No recruiting for a cause. There's room for just one goal in a discipleship relationship: *to disciple another to love Jesus.* Period.

We encourage disciplers to remember Paul's example found in 2 Corinthians 2:17, "Unlike so many, we do not peddle the word of God for profit. On the contrary, in Christ we speak before God with sincerity, like men sent from God."

6. *Disciplers must know when to make referrals*

Disciplers aren't pastors. They aren't counselors. They aren't crisis intervention specialists. If a situation arises that is beyond the ability of the discipler to address, it's time to make a referral to deal with that issue.

Which means, of course, that your church needs to have decided to whom those referrals should be made. Is it the pastor? A para-church organization? Decide before you launch a program so you're ready...and put the information in writing for the people doing discipling in your church.

Keep in mind that should a referral be made, the new believer can address the relevant issue with the pastor (or other designate) while the discipling continues.

7. *Disciplers must stay on task*

We ask disciplers to spend no more than ten minutes at the beginning of each discipleship session chatting about work, family, or other issues. Then it's time to dive into the session.

It may seem odd that on one hand we encourage fellowship and on the other we cut off discussion. It's counter-intuitive, but experience shows us that it's necessary.

A discipleship session—working through the discipleship notebook—is hard work. It takes concentration and effort. It's tempting to spend the hour talking and never geting into the meat of the meeting.

In that way a discipleship session is like a music lesson. If I were learning to play guitar and I had a one-hour lesson each week, what's the best use of that hour? I may love spending time with my guitar teacher, but ultimately I'm better served to spend all hour focusing on my playing. That's where I'll get the information I need to improve.

8. *Disciplers need to meet with new believers in one-on-one sessions*

Group settings (like new member classes or small group sessions) are far less effective than one-on-one sessions for discipleship. Chapter 12 examines this issue in detail, but for purposes of this list, it's sufficient to say that one-on-one is the way to go. Which means that it's very difficult to disciple more than one person at a time.

9. *Disciplers work with new believers of the same* **sex: men with men and women with women**

The reasons are obvious: there's an intimacy that develops between disciplers and new believers. The last thing you want to do with your program is provide temptations for participants.

There have been times that we've had couples disciple couples and it's worked well. But generally speaking, keep the sessions one-on-one rather than in groupings.

10. *Disciplers shouldn't try to solve a new believer's problems*

It may emerge during a discipleship session that a new believer is experiencing financial pressure or needs help in another way. Generally speaking, a discipler should not respond to a need that requires a gift of money, time, or additional resources beyond the discipleship sessions. At least, not without consulting with church leadership.

The reason is that a new believer is already relying heavily on one Christian. Resources to meet legitimate needs will flow through the church—but that means the *whole* church. And the sooner the discipleship sessions have ended, the sooner the new believer will be in a small group that can respond to needs.

A second consideration: when a discipler is both a discipler and the emergency baby-sitter or house painter, it clouds the discipleship relationship. Is the new believer faithful to attend sessions because of a sincere desire to grow or because she feels an obligation to the discipler?

When a concern about money, health, or other issue is pressing, disciplers should call church leadership and see if an avenue to help is open.

11. *And, as mentioned, disciplers are expected to wrap up within three months*

But what about *after* the three months? Can you stay friends?

Absolutely—but we suggest you don't re-enlist as a discipler for the same person, and here's why: you've done what you can. Even if you've become friends, it's time for the person you're discipling to make *additional* enduring relationships—usually in the context of a small group. You'll serve the person you're discipling best if you act as a bridge between that person and the larger church.

Help the person you're discipling connect with a ministry team. Help the person select a small group that will fit his or her needs. Be an encourager as he or she enters into healthy relationships with more Christians.

That's the last task for a discipler: be sure the new believer is in a relationship with others who love Jesus.

Listen—if you stick with the program, you can cover what needs to be covered in weekly meetings over the course of three months. That's truly all it takes—and it's healthiest if you stay on track and complete the discipling in that amount of time.

And then there's you.

No matter how long you've been a Christian, you need people in your life who encourage and challenge you. That's true whether you've been a pastor for thirty years or a layperson for three.

Maybe "mentoring" is a better word than "discipling" when you're already grounded in the faith. But the point remains: you need accountability and encouragement.

Who's providing it?

You see, *everyone* needs a coach, no matter how successful he is walking with Jesus, dunking a basketball, or ripping up a swim medley. Everyone needs a coach, no matter how long she's been spiking volleyballs, shooting skeet, or winning races.

Everyone needs a coach—everyone.

Even Mark Spitz.

Swimming lesson #5

If you weren't around to watch the Summer Olympics in 1972, you didn't see Mark Spitz set the record for the most gold medals won in a single Olympic Games. He took home seven of them.

That's right: *seven.*

During that summer the best swimmers in the world couldn't touch Spitz. He absolutely dominated the events in a way no one had before…and no one has since.

In the world of competitive swimming Spitz was, as they say, The Man.

Yet Spitz is quick to credit "100 percent" of his success in the Olympics to a series of coaches who turned a good swimmer into a great one, and a great one into a legend.[3]

Coach George Haines worked with Spitz during his formative teenage years, when raw talent had to be molded into a disciplined style. Haines saw that Spitz was capable of remarkable things, so he grounded his star swimmer in the basics and then made certain Spitz met the premier collegiate swimming coach in the country.

At Indiana University, "Doc" Counsilman became Spitz's coach.

The Indiana University men's team was a swimming powerhouse. It took six consecutive NCAA Men's Swimming and Diving Championships from 1968 to 1973 and won 20 consecutive Big Ten titles.[4] In the 1964 and 1976 Summer Olympics, his swimmers won 21 of 24 gold medals. Counsilman brought out the best in swimmers.

In addition to fine-tuning Spitz's technique, Counsilman helped the young swimmer deal with earlier losses that impacted Spitz's swimming. Counsilman, a former champion swimmer himself, worked with Spitz on the *mental* part of the sport.

When the Olympics came, Sherm Chavoor served as Spitz's personal coach. He kept Spitz razor sharp and focused through the media storm surrounding Spitz.

Spitz was coached — discipled, if you will — by three very different

coaches, each of whom contributed something unique to Spitz's success. And note that, to be effective, these coaches had to come into
Spitz's development in the precise order and time that they arrived.

As a high school swimmer, Spitz couldn't have absorbed the finer
points that Counsilman had to offer. Spitz just wasn't ready. And had
Spitz's high school coach shown up at the Olympics to remind Spitz
that he needed to remember to look at ceiling tiles during the backstroke, it would have been a wasted trip.

Coaching happens the same way in our spiritual lives. God brings
mentors into our lives at various times, and often those mentors have
precisely the counsel and example we need.

We're never truly finished with being discipled. We've always got
something else to learn…if we're open to learning it.

Who's your coach these days? Who's your mentor?

Exit Pastor John

Like most discipleship relationships, the intensity of my relationship with Pastor John diminished as I grew up in my ministry. I quit
needing his advice as often, and he was wise enough to let me stretch
my wings and take some solo flights.

As I write, we still live in the same town, and we still have high
regard for each other. He's 94 years old, and I have high regard for
anyone who lasts that long, especially in the ministry. The man has
been doing something right—and he's done it right for a very long
time.

It's wise to place limits on discipleship relationships. We've learned
through experience drawing some lines and sticking with them keeps
things healthy, so take seriously the Commonsense Guidelines listed
above. But that's playing defense, making sure a discipler won't be
swallowed up by a needy person being discipled.

There's another piece to the puzzle, and it's this: when young
Christians (or pastors) mature and move on, we feel the loss.

I have grown children, and as much as I wanted them to become the godly young people they now are, making their own decisions and serving God, it was hard to let go.

I liked Daddy hugs. I liked good night kisses. I liked my little ones thinking of me as a hero. Yet all of that was on the way somewhere else: seeing them move on and live adult lives.

Still, I can't page through family photo albums (among the few things that weren't lost when our house caught fire and burned down) without growing tearful. They may be grown up, but I'm still their Daddy. Always will be.

And Pastor John, who helped launch me in ministry and cement my relationship with Jesus, will always be a respected mentor. We may disagree about some issues—and we do, by the way—but he'll always have my ear.

And he'll always feel the loss when he considers that I no longer need him as I once did.

Actually, he may just be glad I've moved on, that I'm not constantly interrupting him with endless questions. I haven't had the courage to call and ask.

 SINK OR SWIM QUESTIONS

- *Knowing it will ground a new believer in the faith, how willing am I to commit an hour a week for three months to discipling that new believer?*

- *Which of the "Commonsense Guidelines" cause me concern? Why?*

- *Who is mentoring you in your faith? Who would you select if you could pick anyone to fill this role?*

Prayer

Dear God, I'm clearly a work in progress. You're renewing my heart and mind, bringing me to a place where I care about what you care about and value what you value. Please keep working with me to mold me. Show me who you'd have coach and mentor me right now, and give that person a heart to cooperate with your purpose in shaping me. Oh—and who are you wanting me to disciple? Where can I serve you in that way?

I'll be looking for your answers, faithful Father. Amen.

11

~~~~

Similar Temptations

Wherein we find there are specific temptations
new believers are likely to encounter…so be prepared.

The Boy Scouts said it best: be prepared.

That's especially good advice when a swimmer moves out of the safety of the pool and into open water.

Consider Scott Coleman, who at forty-one decided to swim the English Channel.

The Channel is the Mount Everest of open water swimming. Currents are strong and often work against you. The water is 60 degrees. From Dover, England, to Cap Gis-Nez, France, it's twenty-one miles of choppy, unpredictable water.[1] And depending on when you start and how well you swim, you may be forced to do at least part of the swim in disorienting darkness.

Coleman did his best to prepare for the challenge. He'd been a competitive swimmer in high school and college and put aside a year for serious training. Four mornings each week he was in the water before 5:00 a.m., swimming for an hour and a half. Afternoons he swam another ninety minutes. He lifted weights and began training in the ocean off Fort Lauderdale—swimming two miles, then three, then six.[2]

He allowed himself just two days off per month.[3]

When Coleman plunged into the waves in England, he was as prepared as possible — well-trained, accompanied by a team of experts, suited, greased, and ready to go.

It took Coleman 11 hours and 54 minutes to reach the beach in France; in the process he lost fifteen pounds and nearly froze to death.[4] The vast majority of even strong swimmers couldn't possibly have completed that course; it's simply too difficult.

But for Coleman — who's a diabetic, by the way — what was impossible became doable...*because he was prepared for the challenge.*

Living the Christian life looks impossible to new believers, too. They think about how often and thoroughly they've fallen short of God's standards, and they just know they're doomed to fail. They can't possibly live the life God has called them to live.

And in some ways they're right.

They *won't* be perfect. They *won't* live a sin-free life.

Consider these words from 1 John.

> *If we claim to be without sin, we deceive ourselves and the truth is not in us. If we confess our sins, he is faithful and just and will forgive us our sins and purify us from all unrighteousness. If we claim we have not sinned, we make him out to be a liar and his word has no place in our lives.*
> —1 John 1:8-10

Those are among the most reassuring words in Scripture. With confession comes forgiveness; we haven't enlisted in a "one strike and you're out" program. New Christians, old Christians, we're all in the same boat: when we sin, if there's authentic repentance, there's heartfelt forgiveness.

Still, just *experiencing* temptation can derail a young believer. It's important new believers be prepared for that tug toward sin, that reminder of the old life.

Our Life Issues virtually guarantee temptation is coming, but there are other temptations, too. And in my thiry years of discipling others, I've noticed that some of them are remarkably common—and seem to come almost like clockwork. I call them "Similar Temptations," and it's wise to prepare to address them in the lives of people you're helping learn to love Jesus.

There is something remarkable about these seven temptations: they appear in new Christians everywhere. I've seen them pop up in Cuba, Russia, Africa, the United States…it's like watching babies go through the same development issues no matter where they're born.

Knowing that these will appear to the people you're discipling helps you keep the discipleship process relevant—and timely. There's a reason parents don't attempt to teach calculus to two-year olds, and there's a reason we don't teach the finer points of pre-tribulation, pre-millennialism to new believers.

The temptation to be discouraged

The Christian life often starts like one of those firework displays Americans flock to see on Independence Day.

There's a barrage of eye-opening blasts and sizzles; the crowd presses close and "oohs" and "ahhhs." Then, after one last fusillade, it's over. All that's left is a fading trail of smoke and the sharp, lingering scent of gunpowder.

People pack up their picnic baskets and wander back to their cars. By midnight the park that was so packed with excitement is nothing more than an open, grassy field.

There's an emotional letdown after something so momentous, whether it's a firework display, a play-off game, or a conversion experience. And when we're talking about the latter, soft voices begin to whisper…

"What will the guys say when they find out I'm a church-goer?"

"What if these church people knew what I was *really* like?"

"Can I quit drinking and doing drugs? And what if I can't?"

There's no end to the questions...and reminders of sins committed. Add to that the confusion new believers often experience about whether they've committed the "unforgivable sin" or whether the Bible is truly reliable, and the first few days after conversion are a mine-field of discouraging thoughts.

That's why it's so critical that new believers begin being discipled *immediately*. Don't be fooled by the euphoria you often see in their faces after church; doubt and discouragement that come with it *will* show up...usually when those new Christians are alone.

Part of the commitment a discipler makes in the *First Steps* program is to be available to provide encouragement when that first moment of discouragement appears for new believers. It's essential that when discouragement rears its head that a discipler stand beside a new Christian to call the discouragement what it is: a temptation to sin.

My first moment of discouragement came the day after I became a Christian. Having been raised in a church, I knew there was something called the "unforgivable sin." I figured since I'd done so much so wrong for so long, I'd probably hit that sin, too. If so, what was the point of my new found faith?

I took aside the guy who'd led me to the Lord and asked him to explain precisely what the "unforgivable sin" was.

I can still remember what he said: "Grant, don't worry about that sin. If you can confess a sin, God can forgive it. The unforgivable sin is when someone becomes so hardhearted that they can't—or won't—confess sin anymore."

Whew! What a relief!

Two years ago I got to be on the receiving end of that question... and it was anything but comfortable.

I was teaching *First Steps* in a prison when a man who had committed two murders asked me, "What's the unforgivable sin? Can God really forgive me?"

Everyone in that crowded room was listening, silently wondering the same thing: Could God really forgive them? Would he?

I shared what I'd been told thirty years earlier. "If you can confess it, God can forgive it."

There are several wonderful Bible passages that address discouragement. I've learned them—I suggest you do, too.

> *The Lord will rescue me from every evil attack and will bring me safely to his heavenly kingdom. To him be glory for ever and ever. Amen.*—2 Timothy 4:18

> *If we confess our sins, he is faithful and just and will forgive us our sins and purify us from all unrighteousness.*—1 John 1:9

Be prepared.

The temptation to surrender to sin

We're guilty of the worst sort of marketing: the bait and switch. We tell people that when someone makes a commitment to follow Jesus, everything changes, that life is fulfilling and joyful, that the skies open and God looks down from Heaven, pleased and applauding.

And it's true that everything changes...except for the stuff that doesn't.

Small wonder that when a new believer finds himself still wanting to fire up the computer and visit a porn site, he's confused. Wasn't Jesus supposed to take all that away? Isn't he redeemed and reborn? What went wrong with the surgery?

You and I know that Christians continue to fail. We know that repentance and forgiveness pave our way back to God.

New believers *don't* realize that—because they haven't learned it yet.

Again—that's why discipling is so valuable. It keeps new believers from deciding that yes, maybe Jesus changes other people, but they personally must have been too far gone to redeem.

So why even try?

Be prepared.

The temptation to live in fear instead of love

The ultimate goal of discipling is to teach someone to love Jesus and, by extension, to love God.

That's got to be taught because very few people enter into a relationship with God motivated by love. Instead, they're motivated by fear.

Fear of Hell. Fear of being alone and without friends like those they met at church. Fear of death. Fear of living a life without hope.

Fear…not love.

Fear is a very intense, very short-lived emotion. It fades quickly, and if a new believer doesn't move from fear to love, some bad things happen.

• *That new believer can simply walk away,* realizing the God she feared isn't actually waiting to zap her with a lightning bolt. It's like a swimmer in Ohio being terrified of being attacked by sharks while swimming. It doesn't take long to realize that, when you're a thousand miles from the ocean, there's no need to be looking over your shoulder for fins on a regular basis.

• *A new believer may not walk away but instead become very, very good at The Rules.* When Christians learn doctrine but not love, they become legalists. There's no life in legalism, just a reliance on rules instead of grace…and that's one of the things for which Jesus died to *free* us.

• *A new believer may join a cult.* This isn't a hollow warning; it happens often. That's because many cults—Jehovah's Witnesses and Mormons, specifically—have proactive discipleship programs. They're committed to it—and many Christian churches aren't.

New Christians are especially vulnerable to cult teaching. These believers have a spiritual awakening but zero ability to discern between what's true and what's false doctrine. How can they? They haven't been taught anything. They aren't in a growing, loving relationship with God.

That's why we disciple quickly—before The Rules become more attractive than a relationship.

Be prepared.

The temptation to be bitter about unfulfilled expectations

Many people come to God as a sort of last resort. Their lives are collapsing, their relationships broken, and they need help—fast. Believing that commiting their lives to Jesus will instantly change things, they walk down the aisle, pray the prayer, and then...return home to find they're still evicted, their car still won't start, and they're still bankrupt.

What happened? Why didn't God come through?

He did...just not as new Christians expect.

The disappointment and bitterness that comes from unfulfilled expectations are the leading reason new believers walk away from faithfulness. And you know what? In our desire to "market" the benefits of salvation, we often contribute to those unrealistic expectations!

The best way to calibrate expectations and process confusion about them is in a one-on-one discipleship relationship. Another good reason to involve a new believer in discipling immediately.

Be prepared.

The temptation to confuse God's will

Remember your first day at a new job? You're clueless—and it shows. You can't find things. You aren't certain what's important and what's just nice to know. You may even do things that are counter-productive—though your heart was in the right place.

New Christians are like that. They're brimming with enthusiasm and passion, so they dive right in. That's admirable—but sometimes ill-informed. They read about fasting and decide that if forty days was good for Jesus, it's good for them, too. They hear a sermon about Jesus returning and decide to quit their jobs, devote themselves to prayer, and let other people support them. That last one's not a new idea, by the way—consider Paul's words to some folks in a church who had watched him earn a living as a tradesman while he worked with them.

> We did this, not because we do not have the right to such help, but in order to make ourselves a model for you to follow. For even when we were with you, we gave you this rule: "If a man will not work, he shall not eat."
> —2 Thessalonians 3:9-10

Discipling helps new believers enter into a relationship with Jesus and start to recognize his voice. They develop discernment and begin to see what God is doing in their lives. They learn to trust God so there's no need to panic when a circumstance or situation is challenging.

New believers won't ever know much about God's will without knowing God. Reading the Bible isn't enough; there has to be relationship.

Be prepared.

The temptation to set unwise priorities

Priorities have to be set—frequently. Welcome to life.

But how can new believers set those priorities *wisely*?

Some new Christians are paralyzed by the task of reorganizing their lives after a decision to follow Jesus. Some stuff is obvious: if you were selling drugs for a living before becoming a Christian, it's important you get work doing something else *after* becoming a Christian.

But what about the more subtle things? Friends? Activities? Life direction?

New believers want to make changes that honor God. Sometimes they panic and change *everything* (which convinces friends and family they've lost their minds) or they change the *wrong* things.

For instance, one new Christian who'd been abusing alcohol and stealing decided that he should give up smoking. He figured he'd start there and then make other adjustments later.

Giving up smoking was probably a good idea. But given the rest of his life, it wasn't exactly the top priority.

When new believers enter into a loving relationship with Jesus, they find that their priorities just naturally begin reflecting Matthew 6:33: "But seek first his kingdom and his righteousness, and all these things will be given to you as well."

That's the gold standard for setting priorities, and it can't really happen apart from a relationship with God. Until the relationship is in place, you can't receive the kingdom or the righteousness.

New believers are often quick to set priorities in strange ways, for all the right reasons. Be prepared.

The temptation to stay insulated

A new believer has been pulled out of deep water, revived, and toweled off. He's safe in the warmth of fellowship. From where he sits, he's completed the journey. All he has to do is sit tight until Jesus comes back or he dies—and then it's Heaven.

Well…not exactly.

In reality, he's been rescued so he can participate in a larger rescue operation. As tempting as it is just to retire, he's drafted into action—

and the best time to start is immediately.

What Jesus observed during his ministry on earth is just as true today.

> *Do you not say, "Four months more and then the harvest?" I tell you, open your eyes and look at the fields! They are ripe for harvest. Even now the reaper draws his wages, even now he harvests the crop for eternal life, so that the sower and the reaper may be glad together.* —John 4:35-36

The temptation to stay on the sidelines is a temptation to sin. Jesus prayed for workers in the harvest field. There's work to do—now. There are people to reach—now. And that's one benefit of having a discipleship program like *First Steps* in your church: it sends workers into the field to harvest souls.

Sharing the Gospel with and discipling others cements the lessons a new disciple has learned. It helps that new believer experience joy. And it grows the fellowship of believers.

I've noticed that when we had ten qualified disciplers, God sent ten new believers our way. When we got to a hundred qualified disciplers, God kept them busy, too. I can't wait to get to a thousand disciplers.

It's going to happen: some new disciples will want to sit out the rest of the race.

Don't let it happen.

 SINK OR SWIM QUESTIONS

• *Which of the Similar Temptations did you deal with early in your Christian life? What was helpful in getting past them? Or — if you're still dealing with them — what would be helpful?*

• *How would a discipleship program in your church address these Similar Temptations?*

Prayer

Dear God, I don't want to be ineffective in serving you. Please help me handle the temptations in my life through your power, not just my own. And if I can be of help supporting others as they encounter these Similar Temptations, give me eyes to see what I can do. Amen.

12

~~~~

One-on-One Culture

*Where you'll determine the discipling culture
of your church and consider how shifting
to a One-on-One Culture might benefit your church.*

Every church has its own culture, its own way of getting things done. And that includes how churches approach evangelism and discipleship.

Let me be clear here: I'm not suggesting there's just one right way to share the Gospel. I responded to the Gospel when some hippies on a Florida beach explained God's love in a way that made sense to me. I know other people who responded in a Sunday school class, at a Vacation Bible School, and while a buddy was leading a Bible study.

God works in many ways, and I never want to put him in a box.

But I *do* want to suggest that if you want your church to move past evangelism and get to discipleship, there's a preferred culture in which that can happen.

We call it a "One-on-One Culture."

Before I describe it, let me describe some other church cultures that may sound familiar. See if any of them describe your church.

The Four Spiritual Laws Culture. This culture values communicating clear, simple Bible truth and eliciting a response. **Favorite question**: "If you died today, would you go to heaven?"

Once someone's prayed the prayer, he or she is told to find a faithful church in which to grow. Often the person presenting the Gospel has no idea if the new convert ever makes that connection. Evangelism is largely disconnected from discipleship. Discipleship happens when the new convert takes the step to go to a church and plug in.

The Small Group Culture. This culture values establishing relationships with people, often with an agenda to engage those people in a discussion about the Gospel. **Favorite question**: "Would you like to meet with a group of others who are considering spiritual issues/ building a stronger marriage/raising children?"

When friends or neighbors make a faith commitment, they're integrated into the larger church that organized the small group. Evangelism and discipleship are linked, though there may or may not be intentional discipling that happens once the new Christian is ushered into the church building.

The Relational Evangelism Culture. This culture values leveraging personal relationships to share the Gospel. **Favorite question**: "How about joining me this Sunday at church?"

You might think this culture of connectivity would be a powerful launching pad for discipleship, but it seldom is. It's usually considered "mission accomplished" if a contact comes to church and accepts Jesus as their Savior.

The High-Impact Program Culture. This culture has mastered the art of hosting a concert, producing a play, or sponsoring a big-name speaker who'll share the Gospel in a powerful way. **Favorite question**: "Would you like a free ticket to a spectacular event?"

People who respond by going forward fill out cards to provide follow-up information and are given a bit of advice to tide them over: read the Bible, pray, and tell someone else what you've done.

Any of these sound familiar? If so, put a check mark next to that type of culture.

Now let's confirm your diagnosis.

Put yourself in the shoes of Nancy, a woman who comes to your church next Sunday and who responds to the Gospel. She's identified herself as wanting to become a Christian, bowed her head, prayed for forgiveness, and she's just opened her eyes.

I can guarantee there's a question she'd love to have answered. That question is: "Now what?"

How your church answers Nancy's question says a lot about how you feel — *really* feel — about discipleship and spiritual growth.

Let's assume the attendance at your church is somewhere north of three or four hundred. If that's the case, I can tell you what *won't* happen: Nancy won't spend much time with the pastor.

I'm the Senior Pastor at our church, and Sunday just after worship service is the absolute worst time possible for you to expect me to have a meaningful conversation with you. I just can't — there's always a line of people who want to connect with me and a long list of things I need to accomplish.

Pastors may shake a new convert's hand on Sunday, but that's about it.

What usually happens for new converts is one of the following:

• *They're told to go to a specific place in the sanctuary after the closing prayer.* Once they're there, someone tells them about a class where they and some other new converts can get helpful information. The class will start in a week…or two…or a month.

• *They're handed a Bible, a book, and maybe a brochure.* No class, but the new convert is told if he'll attend church faithfully and do what's in the book, all will be well.

• *New converts provide contact information and are told someone will call…eventually.* Maybe that call will arrive promptly on Monday, but even *that* is too long for a new believer who's just made an emotional, life-changing decision—a decision that may have separated her from her friends and made her former life the worst possible place to return.

• ***They're warmly greeted...and then forgotten.*** This may be the saddest option. Now that they've responded to the Gospel, it's between them and God to work out the rest of the journey.

That "plunk" sound you just heard was Nancy being tossed into the deep end of the pool to sink or swim on her own.

Compare that to what happens at our church—and yours, if you launch a *First Steps* program.

When Nancy finishes praying, she'll literally be *surrounded* by people who are eager to help her get grounded in the faith. They've been discipled themselves and are trained and willing to disciple someone else. Once Nancy identifies herself as a new believer, those people will find her—and find her fast.

By the way, all those people will be women. Discipling in our church happens in same-sex partnerships. Nancy, who happens to be twenty-three and beautiful (did I mention that?), won't feel as if all the single guys at the church are trying to get dates disguised as discipleship sessions.

As the pastor, I don't worry about new converts finding a discipler. It'll happen because a One-On-One Culture is alive and well at our church. It's our default setting, the way we're wired.

If you make a public faith commitment or join our church, I can guarantee that someone will approach you and say, "If you'd like, I'll walk you through the basics of the faith. Here's a Bible and some material to review, but before you look at either, answer these two questions:

"Do you have any questions about what you just did? If so, let's talk about that right now.

"If not, let's get together this week. What time works best for you?"

That's One-On-One Culture.

What are the benefits of One-On-One Culture?

There are several, but the first may be the most powerful: a One-On-One Culture provides real-world examples of what you are teaching.

One-On-One Culture delivers models

When the disciples who Jesus gathered about him had a question about what pleasing God looked like, they didn't have to search long for an answer. Jesus was right there.

Was serving and healing someone on the Sabbath more important than the ritual that had grown up around the day? Absolutely — Jesus did it.

Were forgiveness and compassion companions of the Law? Sure — Jesus demonstrated how they fit together.

Was heartfelt, stumbling prayer more powerful than empty but eloquent words? Yes — and Jesus said so.

My point: the disciples had an example for godly living. Right there. In the flesh.

I want to be careful about suggesting *you* might be as capable an example of God-pleasing living as Jesus was, but *he's* not here in the flesh…and *you* are.

New believers know they have to change, but they often aren't sure how — or where they want to start. They know they want to follow Jesus, but he's simply not visible.

So they begin following someone they believe is following Jesus.

That can be a good thing. New believers often imprint on the person who led them to Jesus, and nearly always that means they're following someone who at least values evangelism. But it doesn't mean that model cares about ongoing, intentional discipleship.

When there's a discipling culture—a One-on-One Culture—the imprinting happens with a discipler who actively cares for the new believer. The new believer is established seeing it as normal to invest in the lives of others. There's a pattern set: *let God use you to bless the lives of others.*

That's a culture that opens up some tremendous growth in a local church because people committed to discipling are always on the lookout for ways they can connect with others.

Here's how that desire to connect looked on a recent Sunday at our church.

Gail is a woman in her early '60's, and she's always been fairly quiet. She's involved and has a vital faith, but she's not the one you'll see pushing her way into the spotlight.

Gail happened to see a person she didn't know walk into the church. The visitor was also a woman, but in her 30's. Gail approached the visitor and asked how she came to be in our church that Sunday morning.

The visitor didn't really know. She hadn't been invited by anyone, hadn't tracked us down in the yellow pages. She'd seen our sign and decided to come.

Gail introduced the visitor to me and said, "She's going to accept Jesus today."

I don't know who was more surprised, the visitor or Gail. Gail's hand shot up to her mouth and she glanced between the visitor and me. "I don't know why I said that," she admitted, blushing. Then she and the visitor went to find a seat.

After my sermon we gave an invitation to respond to the Gospel, and the visitor walked forward. Gail came, too, and prayed with the woman to accept Jesus. Then, as they were leaving, Gail said, "And I'm going to start discipling her this afternoon."

Notice how a willingness to connect with others played out in

Gail's life. She saw a person she didn't know and risked making a personal connection. That's rare. She sat with the visitor. Equally rare in most churches. And she made herself available as a discipler as soon as the opportunity presented itself.

One-on-One Culture is like that. It supports spontaneous responses to needs in people's lives. That's true in discipleship and equally true in prayer, caring for the sick, giving to help others — all sorts of ministry.

One-on-One Culture is where bonding happens best

Classrooms and small groups are wonderful, but they're horrible places to raise babies. Imagine suggesting to a new mother, who's cuddling her newborn after a long labor, that she should hand over the baby so it can be raised in a small group of babies...or in a baby classroom.

Not that something similar hasn't been tried.

There was a time when a baby was sick it was placed in an isolation unit, away from the baby's mother. Now, when a newborn is struggling, the mother is very involved. The touch of that mother is understood as an irreplaceable part of the infant's healing process.

I don't know if you've had children, but the American childbirth experience is a great indication of how relationship is being valued.

When my children were born, I was allowed in the room with the medical staff, but that was it. It didn't even *occur* to me to ask if, when my second daughter was born, my first daughter could come share the experience. I'm sure my request would have been met with a raised eyebrow and a quick call to Social Services to report I was trying to traumatize a child.

As it was, my eldest daughter had to meet her little sister by visiting the hospital during specific hours, and by specific appointment. That's a tough way to bond with a new family member.

Now hospitals have birthing centers that can hold a group the size of a small convention. Want other children present for the birth? No problem—just make sure they leave enough room for the delivery coach and videographer.

Why the huge change in just a decade or so?

It's not that having babies is any less dramatic. A birth may be a miracle of life, but it's a messy miracle. But we've decided that cementing the family relationships is worth the mess. And why not? Families often want to have the experience together. In some ways—long term—it's better for the baby.

Ditto for new disciples. They can collect information in large or small groups, but the bonding will happen best in more intimate settings, in one-on-one relationships.

So provide those from the very start.

One-on-One Culture provides encouragement, admonition, and accountability

You can give information in large groups. If you're a pastor you probably preach the same sermon or teach the same lesson whether you've got 75 people in your audience or 7,500 people in the pews.

But when it comes to dealing with something where people in your audience feel their lives are on the line, the best place to deal with that kind of information is a one-on-one relationship.

It's too easy to hide in a large group, and unless a small group leader is very, very skilled, it's easy to hide there, too.

If you want to deliver effective, appropriate encouragement, admonition, or accountability, you've got to be in a one-on-one relationship.

How do you get to One-On-One Culture?

I'll tell you straight up: moving into this culture will scare some of your people silly. It may scare a few of them away.

Do it anyway.

Let me suggest three practical steps to take.

Pray — and pray specifically

Ask God to give someone in your congregation a heart for discipleship. When God brings them forward, put a copy of this book and a discipleship notebook in their hands. Then connect your disciple with someone who needs discipling.

In three months you'll have two people energized by the notion that they can be planted in a healthy place and be deeply in love with Jesus. Set them free on two new Christians or two old ones who could use the experience.

Meanwhile, *you* set the vision for discipleship in your church. Convince the church leadership to take seriously Jesus' words about discipleship. Share your testimony about the value of intentional discipleship.

And as you go, pray. Specifically.

Look for opportunities to share your faith — and your friendship

I've noticed that people who've caught a vision for discipleship tend to get chances to share their story and the story of Jesus. These are people who recognize that when they enter into a conversation about religion with the barista at Starbucks or when they run into old friends they haven't seen for twenty years; it's no coincidence.

People who've bought into discipleship are quick to know when it's appropriate to speak into a situation. When it's the right moment to invite someone to church. When it's acceptable to ask someone if he or she needs prayer.

And disciplers know it's always a time to listen.

If you want a culture where people matter, you've got to model that behavior and that attitude.

A church with a One-on-One Culture typically is amazingly friendly and hospitable. People hang around to talk together. The parking lot is always a challenge between Sunday morning services because people in the first service aren't in a hurry to bolt out the door. When someone asks, "So how you doing?" there's a long pause as the person asking waits for an authentic answer. There's spontaneous giving and serving.

Can't picture that kind of atmosphere at your church? Then model it next Sunday — and every Sunday after that.

Finally, remember to pray — specifically

I know, I know, I already mentioned that...but it's worth another mention. You can't change the corporate culture of your church — but God can. And he's looking for people like you to cooperate with his desire to turn your church into a place that's warm...inviting...and discipled into service and love for him.

 ## SINK OR SWIM QUESTIONS

• *So — what's your church culture? Four Spiritual Laws? Small Group? Relational Evangelism? High-Impact Program? Or are you already a One-on-One Culture?*

• *In what ways do you agree — or disagree — that a One-on-One Culture is best for your church?*

Prayer

Dear God, I want our church to reflect your Kingdom. I know your will is that we value what you value, care about what you care about... and that means we need to care deeply about people. Give my church leadership a heart for discipleship and seeing those who know you grow strong in the faith. Give me a heart for the same gracious God. Amen

13

~~~~

Obedience

*How the ultimate discipleship discipline – obedience
– enabled me to hear God, make good decisions, and get the girl.*

We've looked at four essential disciplines of discipleship: prayer, Bible study, fellowship, and evangelism/discipleship. But there's another discipline that comes first. It's less a discipline than a decision, I think; a decision that's lived out in lots of ways.

It's a decision to be obedient to Jesus. And obeying Jesus is a lot easier when you have a base of specific prayer and Bible study.

Discipleship comes with a price tag

When Jesus called his disciples into relationship with him, he made it abundantly clear it wasn't going to be all wine and lilies of the field.

> *Blessed are you when people insult you, persecute you
> and falsely say all kinds of evil against you because of me.
> Rejoice and be glad, because great is your reward in heaven,
> for in the same way they persecuted the prophets who were
> before you.* — Matthew 5:11-12

There was going to be a cost of being a disciple—a high cost. But then again, it came with a substantial benefit, too.

> *For whoever wants to save his life will lose it, but who-*
> *ever loses his life for me will find it. What good will it be for*
> *a man if he gains the whole world, yet forfeits his soul? Or*
> *what can a man give in exchange for his soul?* —Matthew
> 16:25-26

Somehow, the church has turned over describing discipleship to the marketing department. We're all about spelling out the benefits of knowing Jesus, and any discussion about the cost...well, that gets buried in the fine print.

And as a pastor, I'm not without blame here. We pastors do it all the time. "Come to Jesus just as you are," we say, forgetting the part where he's not expecting you to *stay* just as you are.

We're big on talking about Jesus the Savior.

We don't mention as often Jesus the Lord.

But *they're the same person.* You can't have a relationship with Jesus the Savior—the one who died on the cross and who loves you enough to rescue you from sin—without also entering into relationship with Jesus the Lord.

And he's the one who expects a few things from you. He may love you unconditionally, but he plans for you to get with the program, too.

And in a word, that program is "obedience."

Fan or disciple?

Until someone obeys Jesus, that person isn't really a disciple.

He's more like a fan who enjoys attending the concert, wearing the t-shirt, and bragging that he's got the drummer's cell phone number. He's there for the big show but doesn't stick around to carry out the equipment and sweep out the stands.

Disciples do more. They're committed. They take direction and do as they're told. And if that sounds oppressive, please don't misunderstand: it's not. Jesus expects his disciples to listen and obey, but he calls them to do things that are ultimately for their own good and God's glory.

The four foundational discipleship disciplines we covered are powerful—they'll get new converts (and old ones who've never quite plugged in) planted where they'll be nurtured through a relationship with Jesus. That's all good.

But all the Bible study in the world won't make a bit of difference unless a disciple is willing to—out of love for Jesus—obey what God's Word tells him to do. All the fellowship that a thousand potluck dinners can offer won't change a disciple's behavior if she's not willing to obey Jesus.

Obedience is bedrock…and it requires a decision.

Will a disciple obey—or not?

Our obedience won't be perfect, of course; there will still be stumbling and sin. But obedience is a default setting for disciples. They may not be wearing "What Would Jesus Do?" bracelets, but they're constantly asking a version of the question. They face life asking, "What would you have me do, Jesus?"

I wish I could tell you that obedience is a clear-cut thing. It's not. Sometimes we don't know exactly what to do. Other times our emotions get in the way of seeing what's the obedient response, what God wants us to do.

And sometimes we're just plain sinful and stubborn.

As a pastor for the past thirty years, I've had a front-row seat as people have made decisions—both good and bad ones. I've watched young people get married, have children, become grandparents, and live out a life filled with the blessings that come with making consistently good decisions.

I've also listened to people sob with regret after making a series of mistakes and bad decisions.

Not long ago, a middle-aged man sat in my office, blinking back tears. He'd recently been fired from his job. His wife had left him years before, and his children wouldn't speak to him. He was on the verge of bankruptcy.

When I suggested to this man that he should live his life by following Jesus, he said, "I don't think it's the right time for me to make that decision."

Um…right.

Good decisions come in all sizes. I've watched a man quickly shut the door to his hotel room when he answered a knock and found a prostitute waiting in the hall. I've seen a teenager decide that popularity wasn't worth doing drugs. I know a business owner who consistently uses his prosperity to help the poor. And my wife often encourages me to pull into Starbucks for coffee—I always count that as a good decision, too.

But the best decisions all fit into one category: *they're decisions that reflect our obedience to God.*

Decisions, discipleship, and obedience

Decisions have the ability to shape our lives. They set us on paths that can be difficult to leave, paths that take us places we never intended to go.

When I talk to prison officials about teaching discipleship to inmates, I'm invariably asked what the benefits will be. I say, "These guys have made some bad decisions; I'm going to teach them how to make good decisions."

That's often enough to convince prison officials that *First Steps* is a worthwhile program. Wardens know only too well the consequences of poor decisions.

A disciple of Jesus has to make decisions just like everyone else.

Where to go to school, what to wear to the job interview, when to take out the trash. Some decisions are so trivial that you hardly notice making them.

Other decisions are clearly huge—and perhaps frightening. We want to make good decisions—wise ones that will prove beneficial—but we're not quite sure what to do. We don't know the future. We can't tally up all the pros and cons.

And, if we're disciples, what we want most is to obey God's will, to honor him, and to make the call he wants us to make. That requires obedience.

Let me walk you through how my decision to be obedient impacted the most important decision I can imagine making, other than to follow Jesus.

It was my decision about who to marry.

The missing bride

When I was nineteen years old I had a disastrous dating experience. I won't go into detail, but be assured if it could go wrong, it did. If it could be misunderstood, it was. If it could rip out my heart and run it through a meat grinder, it did.

Got the picture?

The experience was sufficiently traumatic that several years later, when I was twenty-one, I still hadn't resumed dating. I was doing just fine on my own, thank you. The emotional stitches hadn't all come out yet.

So imagine my surprise when, during a lunch with my mentor, John, he informed me that it was time I found someone to marry. I nearly choked on my Diet Coke.

"Why would you say such a thing?" I asked.

"You're about to graduate from Bible College," he said. "You won't be as successful in the ministry without the right wife. I think it's time that you found one."

John was still munching his sandwich thoughtfully as I digested what he'd told me. Clearly I needed a bit of clarification.

I said, "Okay, it's time for me to find a wife. What should I look for in a Christian wife?"

I'm not exactly sure what I was expecting this gray-haired pastor to say. Maybe provide a description of the perfect woman — someone holy, dressed so modestly she was hardly visible, and who wouldn't consider sex outside (or perhaps even inside) the vows of marriage.

My problem was that I'd only dated non-Christian women. I had no idea what a Christian wife would look like. Probably a cross between Mother Teresa and Billy Graham…which might explain why I hadn't dated any Christians yet.

John thought for a moment.

"Okay, let me give you five things to look for in a Christian wife," John said. "First, she should be sexually attractive to you."

That's when I *did* choke on my Diet Coke. Sexual attraction wasn't the first thing I expected *Pastor* John would list when describing the perfect Christian wife. John was a *pastor*. Was he even *allowed* to give advice like that?

"Why?" I asked.

John raised an eyebrow, considering perhaps just how hopeless his disciple really was.

"Because you have to *sleep* with her," he said.

I pushed the Diet Coke aside. "Okay, so that's the first thing to look for in a Christian wife. What next?"

"Look at her mother," John said. "When you look at a girl's mother, realize *that* is what you will be married to in thirty years."

So far John hadn't said one thing I expected him to say. He was sort of like Jesus in that way, though I don't recall Jesus ever giving advice to James and John about checking out their dates' mothers.

"Third," John said, "She should be a Christian."

Finally. Finally something that sounded like it should be on the list. "Give the other two," I said, taking notes.

"She should get along well with other women."

Again, I was confused. "Why?"

"Because a woman who doesn't get along with other women, who just has guy friends, will be jealous when you talk to other women. And in the ministry you will have to talk to lots of women."

That made sense. John was giving me a list of the physical, spiritual, and emotional attributes of a perfect Christian wife. An *unorthodox* set of attributes, to be sure, but ones based on his many years in the ministry.

"The final one?" I asked.

"She should be smarter than you."

That one struck me as the easiest of the bunch to find. But still…I asked him to elaborate.

"If two people who get married don't have similar educational backgrounds and intelligence, there's a continued disparity that will cause tension the entire marriage." Then he looked at me, and with a slight smile added, "And in your case, you need someone smarter than you or you'll bully her your entire marriage."

John wasn't being unkind; he knew how strong-willed I was.

I finished writing the list on a napkin, folded it, and tucked it in my pocket.

Time to find a wife!

Checklist

Before my conversation with John, I'd assumed God wanted me to be the celibate St. Francis of Hippiedom, forever proving my allegiance to Jesus by looking the other way when attractive women walked by. But here was Pastor John — man of God, long time pastor, extraordinarily wise dispenser of good advice — telling me to find a wife.

I didn't need any more conviction. Who could say no to an assignment like finding the perfect wife? So with my five-point checklist in hand, I literally began "checking" out the women in my ministry.

A year later, my napkin somewhat tattered and no perfect mate in sight, I was on the edge of despair. Perhaps I should just marry someone I wasn't attracted to; maybe select someone rejected by others to prove my spirituality. But even I could see the problems that would come with signing up for a martyr marriage.

Two thoughts came to mind:

First, if Elijah could command God to summon fire from Heaven (well, maybe it was more like God prompting Elijah to *ask*), then perhaps it was possible to convince God to send a perfect woman my direction. It hadn't happened so far, but I could always keep asking… and looking.

Second, I finally prayed, "God, I can be happy single, and I'm willing to do that if it's your will." That turned out to be a prayer my buddy, Pastor John, endorsed wholeheartedly.

"Grant," he said, "you'll never be happy or ready for marriage until you're happy being single."

It was great knowing that surrendering my future married life to God was the right call, but it still left me single. Which, oddly enough, at last began to feel all right. I was ready to put aside my checklist.

And then I saw her.

Our ministry owned a small farm with a creek running through the back end of the land. When someone wanted to get baptized, we immersed the person in that creek. That night, I was officiating the baptismal service, and as I walked out of the ministry building, heading to the creek, I literally bumped into the girl of my dreams.

Her name was Barbara and I was instantly in love. As I walked with her to the stream, I checked her out — spiritually, of course.

• Was I attracted to her? *Yes!*

• What did her mother look like? *I didn't know, but by the looks of the daughter I was willing to take my chances.*

• Had she also gone to college, and was she smarter than me? *Yes, and almost certainly.*

• Did she get along well with other women? *I wasn't sure, but given her perfect score so far one minor infraction was allowed.*

• Was she a Christian? *No...and this was **not** a minor problem.*

Uh, oh. Not only had I decided to marry a Christian, I'd also promised to never even *date* a non-Christian. My "perfect woman" was in the crosshairs, right in front of me, ready to be named and claimed, and the most important item on my list couldn't be checked off.

Time to call in the heavy artillery: pray that she'd become a Christian.

And since this was serious stuff, I decided to pray *and* fast. No way was I going to let Satan take the perfect woman away from me.

I'd prayed before for a girlfriend, so that wasn't new for me. But praying for a particular woman to become a Christian so she could then become my girlfriend? That was uncharted territory.

It quickly became clear that I actually had two adversaries, not just one. Satan didn't want Barbara to become a Christian, so he was Adversary Number One. My second adversary was my best friend—who also wanted to date Barbara.

Adversary Number Two had actually helped me start the ministry in which we both worked. He was a talented musician, a fine Bible teacher, and worst of all—handsome. Plus, he'd never made a commitment to avoid dating non-Christian women. To him, all women were fair game...including Barbara.

Calling down fire on my best friend

Once I realized Barbara wasn't a Christian, I knew I had to slam the brakes on our relationship then and there. I had my list. I had my commitment.

My friend, on the other hand, had a date. He'd immediately asked

Barbara out, and she'd accepted.

What could I do? I couldn't let my intentions be known. I also knew I couldn't compete with my best friend for Barbara's affections. But I had to do *something*.

I immediately instituted a regimen of moping around and questioning the goodness of God. When that didn't work, I tried making vows—I'd never sin again, I'd up my tithe, I'd suffer for years in Siberia as a missionary—but the vows didn't work, either.

So I tried prayer. I'd learned the principle of specificity, that God answers specific prayers. And knowing specific prayers require that I ask for things that have observable answers, I began to pray for very specific things to happen…

God, bring a plague of lice on my best friend.

God, cause the ground to open up and swallow him whole.

Okay, God, forget the lice. Just take him to Heaven like you took Enoch.

None of those prayers were answered, so I called my discipler, John, and asked him to lunch. I wanted his advice. I told John about my vows and also confessed I'd been praying for rather grim events to occur in the life of my friend.

John smiled. Actually, he laughed out loud. Then he said, "You weren't too far off with one of your prayers."

"Are you telling me God might *really* cause the ground to open and swallow him whole?" I asked hopefully.

"Not that prayer. The other one. The one about God taking someone out of the way."

This was more like it. If I could enlist God's help taking my best friend out of the picture, then there would be plenty of time for Barbara to accept Christ and fall in love with me. It was a plan!

Unfortunately, John continued talking, "I'm not talking about your best friend moving aside," he said. "I'm talking about *you*. If you're eventually going to marry this woman, you have to be willing to walk away now. It will be difficult, but it's the right thing to do. She's a non-Christian and you've said God wants you to only marry a believer. Be obedient to what God wants you to do."

This wasn't what I wanted John to say, but it was exactly what I needed to hear. I was fortunate that God put a discipler in my life who had the courage to tell me the truth…but that doesn't mean I immediately got with the program.

For a few days I continued to wheedle and negotiate with God, and I got zero cooperation. Eventually, griping and groaning, I walked away.

If Barbara and I were going to marry, it was going to take more than my efforts to manipulate God.

And my desire to throw my best friend under a truck.

Obedience helps us know God's will

I appreciated the advice my friend and discipler, John, had given me about finding a wife. But he had given me something else that was far more valuable. John had given me one-on-one discipling that helped me discover the key to knowing God's will.

That key was *obedience*.

God had already made it abundantly clear that I wasn't to be dating a non-believer. So why was I trying to squirm around that clear direction? As a disciple of Jesus, my first priority was to be obedient to God…period.

Let me point out the obvious: I wasn't seeing things clearly on my own.

Life's like that, you know. What seems remarkably clear in hindsight or in the life of someone else is muddied and foggy in our own lives. Had a friend told me the solution to his romance problems was an earthquake swallowing his best friend, I'd have seen his solution for what it was: stupidity.

But from the *inside*, it all seemed perfectly reasonable.

Knowing God's will is a matter of correctly understanding Biblical principles; receiving informed, practical advice; discerning the Spirit of God's leading; and being obedient. It's not often a completely clear-cut thing, and very often it is best pointed out by a friend.

In my case, I perhaps *had* found the right woman to marry...but that wasn't the point. The point was that I'd never have a good marriage until I'd discovered and accepted God's will. Until I was faithful and obedient as a disciple. I had to be willing to walk away from Barbara, willing to turn things over to God.

I'll be the first to admit it didn't feel fair. Why had God seen fit to have me meet Barbara only to then remind me that obedience required I step away? I'd been looking for a year, remember: if God wanted me single, he could have told me earlier.

But the point for a disciple is obedience. Everything else flows out of that.

It's actually a very freeing thing. You see, if you're obedient to God, you aren't responsible for the outcome; he is. Sometimes your obedience leads to the outcome you want (marry Barbara) and other times it leads to what feels like failure (Barbara marries my piano-playing Casanova friend). Either outcome is right so long as it flows out of obedience to God.

The principle of "losing your life" (your ambitions, desires, and resources) for God's sake ultimately to gain your life back is at the very heart of discipleship.

It's a simple lesson to learn — and a challenging one to live.

Want to find God's will for your life? Become a disciple...and obey God.

To find God's will is to find purpose in life. It brings meaning to a Christian's calling and spiritual gifts. Obedience brings a Christian into alignment with God's will.

And here's how it looked in my situation with Barbara.

New York City wasn't Heaven...but it would have to do

Not long after I walked away from Barbara, The-Heaven-Sent Woman, my friend called. He'd won a classical piano contest and was moving along to the next level of the competition. He'd be in New York City for two weeks. I'd asked God to whisk him off to Heaven in Enoch style, and while New York City wasn't Heaven, it was where Barbara wasn't.

New York would have to do.

I had two weeks, and a *lot* to accomplish. Somehow Barbara had to be convinced of the Lordship of Jesus, accept Jesus as Savior, and then fall in love with me. If all that happened—pretty much instantly— then the last item on my list could be checked off, Barbara would be a believer, she'd be interested in me, and I could welcome my friend back from New York with an invitation to play at my wedding.

Simple. Nothing to it. A God who could get all of Israel across the Red Sea should be able to handle my request in two weeks.

So I prayed. And prayed. And nothing happened. I prayed some more. One week passed, the second week started; still nothing. More prayer and no good news.

I was getting desperate. My friend was coming back soon. More prayer.

I was scheduled to speak at a ministry gathering on Friday. I knew Barbara was coming, and it was my last chance before my friend got home.

That week, during my preparation for the message, I felt it was God's will that I give an invitation to respond to the Gospel at the end of my talk. I reviewed all the Billy Graham books in my library and re-memorized several key passages from C.S. Lewis's *Mere Christianity*.

I was ready...right up until I opened my mouth that Friday night. My stumbling message was so muddled that I figured it would be a miracle if somehow my entire audience didn't abandon the Kingdom just so they could avoid spending more time with me.

But one person was listening. One person was convicted. And Barbara accepted the Lord.

I asked Barbara if she wanted to get something to eat to celebrate her decision. She agreed and, at the end of the evening, I told her I wanted to date her. She said yes.

Barbara had become a Christian, expressed an interest in me, and I was dating her—all within two hours. And all before my friend got back to town!

The foundational discipleship discipline: obedience

When Jesus taught the Great Commission, he added an interesting phrase: "…go and make disciples of all nations,…*teaching them to obey everything I have commanded you*" (Matthew 28:19-20, *emphasis added*).

In this sentence Jesus made a clear connection between discipleship and obedience. Discipleship is a relationship in which new believers learn to obey Jesus. That's an essential element of discipling: *to teach believers to obey*.

I've heard missionaries talk about Africa having a spirituality that's "a mile wide and two inches deep." I've heard Christian pollster George Barna bemoan a lack of commitment in Americans who claim to be believers.[1] Europe is a virtual wasteland when it comes to living out the Christian faith. Apparently obedience is an issue no matter what continent you happen to be standing on.

According to Jesus, obedience must be taught. A heartfelt commitment to God's will can only be learned in the context of a relationship. Jesus knew this and commanded his followers to go, disciple, and teach obedience to God's will. It was a package deal.

Why is relationship so essential for learning obedience? Well, think about those youngsters I taught to swim. I didn't have them read a book about swimming. Nor did I have them sit in a classroom as I lectured about the finer points of the flutter kick.

Those kids needed to learn by example and to have someone with them demonstrating the skills they needed to master.

Like swimming, discipleship isn't just about information. It's about transformation—and the opportunity to become enthusiastic about what's being taught.

I love swimming. I love the feel of the water on my skin and the steady, smooth rhythm as I snap off lap after lap. When I'm in the water I'm happy—and that makes helping others learn to swim a joy, too.

As a swimming instructor I'm not just transferring skills and information; I'm inviting others to join me in a world I enjoy. It's my obvious enthusiasm and love of swimming that encourages others to give swimming a try, too.

When an enthusiastic, mature Christian invites a new believer to join him or her in living out the faith—that's motivational. It draws new believers into growth as they hear the testimony of their disciplers and see their disciplers persevere during difficult times.

The love that disciplers have for Jesus is contagious, and soon anyone they're discipling experiences it as well. And *that's* the reason relationships matter in learning obedience: discipleship relationships model a love for Jesus.

Do you need to obey Jesus? Yes—but that obedience has to be there for the right reason. Not because he's more powerful than you (he is) or that he knows what you're thinking (he does) or that he'll be coming back to see you (he will).

The only lasting, ever-fresh motivation for obedience is love.

More in love today than ever

My discipler, John, officiated my marriage to Barbara on July 9, 1977. That was almost thirty years ago. I can honestly say that today I am more in love with my wife than ever.

What we're experiencing today is a different sort of love than we started with back then. It's more satisfying, more informed, and more enduring. Barbara and I were talking recently, and we agreed that while we've enjoyed all the years of our marriage, those first years aren't ones we'd care to repeat.

We were in love then, but it was an immature love. The excitement of launching our life together was wonderful, but there was plenty of turmoil as we figured out the whole "becoming one" process.

After nearly thirty years we now have history together—we've shared the experience of having friends and family members die, coped with living on a pastor's salary, raised three children, traveled the world together, and survived our house burning. We've cried together, laughed together, and at times faced off to yell at each other. We've watched other couples divorce. But we still love one another and look forward to many more years of life together.

It's a truth shared at most weddings: the marriage relationship reflects our relationship with the Lord. Good decisions build the relationship, and bad decisions (sometimes just one) can destroy it. Both Barbara and I come from families that have remained intact. Our parents didn't divorce. We have the advantage of loving Jesus more than the world. And both of us followed biblical principles while we dated.

These advantages have helped our marriage, but our success hasn't been happenstance. We were given a solid foundation by our families, and we were helped along by Pastor John's mentoring. We also benefited from the advice of friends, the prayer of people who love us, and God's grace. We're not claiming credit for surviving as a couple and for raising three remarkable children.

Except for one piece of the puzzle.

We *do* take credit for deciding to love Jesus and be obedient to him. And that's made all the difference in the world.

And my best friend? He did well, too. He went on to fame, success, and even made a fair amount of money as a musician—no small feat, and a testimony to his talent. He also married a wonderful woman and has five children. I don't see him much any longer; our ministries have headed in different directions.

But I do expect to hear from him when he reads how I tried to get God to split his skull with a lightning bolt.

Sorry, friend.

 SINK OR SWIM QUESTIONS

- *What in your life is evidence of your obedience to God?*

- *What in your life is evidence of disobedience?*

Prayer

Dear God, it's tough to see it in black and white: a list of ways we're disobedient to you. Yet, we know it's true—we're not always faithful. We want to serve you from the depths of our hearts, not just go through the motions. Give us a love for you that prompts us to obey you joyfully, to be wholly yours.   Amen.

14

~~~~

Becoming a Discipling Church

The four steps to becoming a church where
discipling happens easily and naturally.

Okay, you're sold.
You see there's a need for authentic, intentional discipling in your church, and you don't see much of it happening. Classes, yes. Preaching, yes. Discipling, no.

Now what? How do you get from where you are to where you want to be?

I want to give you a four-step roadmap to get you to a place where discipling happens easily and naturally in your congregation. I've made the journey myself, so you can trust this map.

And you can also trust that, unless you're willing to take *all* the steps, you'll soon be off track.

Step 1: Address the four foundational principles

Unless you understand and implement the four principles out-lined in this book, you're unlikely to be successful. It's vital you keep these four principles in mind—and in prayer.

• *One-on-One Culture* is your promised land—the place you want to reach as a church culture. Fix it firmly in mind because, as a church leader, you need to paint a vivid picture of where you're headed as a church.

Call it vision-casting if you will; I think of it as a continual process of sending postcards from Hawaii with "wish you were here" scribbled on the back. When people in Ohio get enough of those, they start picturing themselves under palm trees in a sweet evening breeze. They can almost smell the fragrant leis hanging around their necks. Before they know it they've booked tickets and started packing for their trip.

• *Three months* is the amount of time initial discipling requires — trust me. We've tested, tweaked, and tried again and every time we land back at three months.

There are people in your church who believe the essential disciplines of discipleship can be taught in an hour class or a half-day seminar, and to some extent those people are right. The disciplines can be *taught*…but they won't be *learned*.

That is, the new believers won't actually *put into practice* what they wrote down during a lecture. That's not how life-change works or how habits form.

Again: discipleship isn't about transferring information — it's about life transformation. Be willing to invest three months into each discipleship relationship for all the reasons I've discussed.

• *Embrace the foundational disciplines* of specific prayer, specific Bible study, specific fellowship, and specific evangelism. First, decide to engage fully those disciplines in your own life. Discover how God uses them in and through you. Model them for others.

There's no skipping that step, by the way.

God isn't looking for people who have a tremendous theoretical understanding of discipleship. He has all of those he needs. What he wants are disciples who will know, love, and follow Jesus.

Are you willing to be a disciplined disciple yourself? If not, give this book to someone in your church who is.

And embrace journaling as a way to keep track of how God is answering your prayers. That's where you'll begin seeing the pattern of God's consistent love in your life—and the lives of people you disciple.

• *Understand the patterns of similar temptations.* That understanding is what fuels both acceptance when new disciples stumble and a dogged determination to focus growth where it will do the most good. It's what helps new believers sort out what Bible verses to memorize first, what relationships are best left in their old lives, what places they should avoid.

And these four principles are trans-cultural, by the way. No matter where you are, they're essentials. Leave any of them out and discipleship in your church will suffer—if it happens at all.

Step 2: Have the right materials

At our church it's the *First Steps* discipleship notebook—and there are good reasons the same resource should be in your church, too.

A quick disclaimer: you may think that because we created and provide this notebook that we're biased. And you're right—we are. But we're biased because we know it works.

Having one standard training manual for your entire discipleship program gives you advantages you'll wish you had if you move forward without one.

• *You'll know the right material is being covered—in the right order*

It's easy for disciplers to play to their own strengths. If they happen to value prayer and aren't all that interested in Bible study, guess what? They're going to create disciples who value the same things. Prescribed sessions that provide a balanced diet for new believers are a must.

• *You can gauge a discipler's effectiveness*

If at the end of the three-month discipleship session a new believer hasn't mastered the material, you'll know to retrain the discipler before he or she enters into another discipleship relationship.

We don't give people emerging from a three-month discipleship relationship an exit interview to determine how deeply they were impacted, but now that I think of it—it's not a bad idea to spot-check.

• *You don't have to reinvent the wheel*

I'd have given a great deal to have the *First Steps* discipleship notebook when we were first getting started. If you attempt to create a printed resource from scratch, I can guarantee in three to six months you'll be thinking the same thing. The discipleship notebook we provide is biblical, relevant, tailored to this purpose, and field-tested literally thousands of times. Give it a try.

And here's another resource that's a key piece of the discipleship puzzle: you must train your disciplers regarding the nuts and bolts covered in chapter 10. We conduct church-specific seminars that will train and equip a church to become a discipling church in just a day and a half.

We teach the introductory principles, train believers how to disciple others, and then take attendees through a qualification process. Because this is a group session rather than one-on-one teaching, it's appropriate for mature Christians but not new believers who are wanting to get discipled.

But if you're looking to train a number of people in your church in one quick weekend so you've got a group ready to start discipling others, this seminar is for you. Visit our website at www.disciplinganother.com or call us at 937-322-5381 for details.

Step 3: Make discipleship an institutional priority

The church is full of programs. Packed with programs. Sometimes *overwhelmed* with programs. The typical announcement time in some worship services sounds like a network news broadcast.

The bloodmobile is coming Thursday night. The youth group needs volunteers for a short-term mission project. There's a meeting of the Ladies' Retreat Committee after the morning service. AWANA on Wednesday, AA on Monday, YWAM on Sunday night. Film at eleven.

Count up the programs in your church: if there are fewer than thirty I'll be impressed with your laser focus on doing a few things and doing them well.

And in that environment — where people are already busy and getting busier by the moment to keep all the programs up and running — you want to add one more? One that requires a *three-month commitment*?

Well…yes.

Unless you decide that discipleship will be more than just another program, that it will become a primary focus, it's going to get lost in the shuffle.

Here's what you need to make discipleship a priority and, in time, a normative part of your culture:

• ***Make discipleship a shared vision.*** Remember talking about "one-on-one culture" as a promised land? Here's where that comes into play. Find ways to keep the vision alive and in front of people — including through the pulpit, if possible.

• ***Get discipleship into the budget.*** What's funded gets attention — and visibility. The typical process of going to a church board and asking for a budget is a good one — it forces you to plan what you want to do, when you want to do it, and why doing it supports your church's mission statement. It also flushes out who's for discipleship and who talks a good game but really believes it's optional.

• *Ask this question frequently:* *If I placed a recently converted Christian into your care, do you know exactly what to do to maximize the chances of this new Christian maturing in Christ?*

It's a rubber-meets-the-road question…and powerfully demonstrates the status of discipleship in your church. When questioned about the need, or patronized about your passion for discipleship, or simply ignored: ask the question — Loudly — and wait for an answer.

You may not make friends, but you'll be remembered.

• *Find a point person*

Nothing happens without someone taking initiative and organizing your efforts. You need a point person who'll connect people who need discipling with trained disciplers. Who'll administer the program. Who'll carry the vision forward and keep the flame burning bright.

At our church, I'm not that person. Not any more.

As a Senior Pastor I already have plenty on my plate. While I beat the discipleship drum and completely support the program, I've delegated the logistics to others. If you're a Senior Pastor, may I suggest that, as quickly as possible, you do the same?

Two reasons: you're already the point person for so many things; you risk dropping the ball if you're juggling too much.

And second, there's huge credibility that comes with a layperson taking charge of the program. If you're the pastor you're *supposed* to be prodding people to do ministry; it's part of your *job*. You're easily discounted.

But if Mrs. Downing — who caught the vision and it's changed her life — takes the ball and runs with it, who's going to brush her off? She has a testimony that's a powerful story.

• *Have discipling materials readily available*

Stock up now on *First Steps* discipleship notebooks. What you *don't* want is for someone to say, "Well, I'm ready"… and you're not.

At my church, anyone who wants to be discipled receives a free *First Steps* discipleship notebook.

Here's how we do it: when someone is interested in being discipled, we give that person's notebook to his or her discipler. At their first meeting the discipler presents the notebook to the person being discipled.

• *Set a high bar*

As soon as possible, put disciplers through both discipling and a training experience. Qualify disciplers. Take preparation seriously and get ready now. Until you're prepared to disciple new believers, why should God bring many into your church?

I'd encourage you to use the same training we use. Again—it's available from *First Steps* —and it'll give you the benefit of our field-testing and tweaks.

At our church there's a two-step process to become a discipler.

First, a person *must* go through the discipleship process—and that includes people who've been believers for thirty years. We want them to know the power of what they're teaching by receiving it from a trained discipler.

Second, we have a three hour course that trains discipled people how to disciple others. That course is available from us, by the way. Just visit our website (www.disciplinganother.com) or call us (937-322-5381) and we'll tell you how to get it.

Step 4: Pulled, not pushed

Here's what you'll discover discipleship does for you: it dramatically decreases the number of people who just slide through your church building—in the front door and then, in a few months, on out the back. Discipleship causes people to stick because it launches relationships.

But prove that for yourself. Track what happens to new believers (or old ones, for that matter) who are discipled and compare that to people who aren't discipled. It's a sobering revelation.

And ask a question that's harder to quantify: who's joyful in their faith? It stands to reason that people who are loving God and experiencing his love in return will be more joyful than those people who are simply engaged in a religious exercise.

But test it. Ask the hard questions. Let discipleship prove its worth to you, to your church board, and to your congregation.

At some point, when discipling has happened awhile in your church, you'll sense a subtle shift that means everything: the momentum will go from a "push" to a "pull."

A "push" is you—or someone else—constantly pushing the program forward, talking it up, finding ways to make discipleship relationships happen.

A "pull" is when the program has enough momentum that people are actively *seeking* to be involved.

That point may not come quickly. It may take several years. But it *will* come because discipling *is* a function Jesus intends for his Church. And when it comes, you'll be astounded at how members of your church take ownership of the discipleship process. The one-on-one culture you've desired will begin to peek through. It will become business as usual in your church.

And you'll see the energy that comes when Christians see God work through them to influence others. It's a joy to behold.

Congratulations: you're swimming…and you've brought others along with you to the pool.

Sooner or later, every new swimmer decides to try out the diving board.

Once you've mastered the shallow end of the pool and grown comfortable in the deep end, taking a leap off the diving board is the ultimate achievement, the ultimate proof there's no longer a fear of water.

When a dive goes well, it's truly a moment to remember.

When a dive goes poorly, well...*that's* a moment to remember, too.

The good news for beginning swimmers is that if they jump off the diving board, they're pretty much guaranteed to hit water. Gravity takes care of that. If they can define "success" as "climb the stairs, walk out on that little board, and land in water," they'll be successful.

And how you define "successful" can mean everything.

Consider Scott Donie.

Swimming lesson #6

Scott Donie was a 1992 Olympic silver medalist, and in the early 1990's there wasn't another American daredevil diver who was his equal.

Donie was king of the *tough* stuff: ten meter platform diving. That's thirty-three feet in the air by yardstick and about a million feet in the air when you're up there looking down.

Less than a year after bringing home an Olympic medal, Donie was competing at the Olympic Festival in San Antonio. And, as usual, he was blowing away the competition. It was his sixth of ten dives and as the crowd looked up, there was Donie, upside down, fingers clamped to the edge of the diving platform. He was in a classic pose, toes pointed straight up.

The crowd expected to see what they usually see: a diver holds the position for three, maybe four seconds, then pushes off into the dive.

But Donie didn't move.

Five seconds...then ten...then fifteen.

Donie's arms began to quiver.

Twenty seconds...then twenty-five.

What the restless crowd couldn't see, what the judges didn't know, was that Donie was losing his nerve. He was thinking about how it might feel to completely miss his dive and hit the water in a way that injured himself permanently.

Thirty seconds…then thirty five.

Then Donie did the unthinkable: he lowered himself to the platform, turned, and climbed back down the same way he had climbed up.

Donie lost the competition—but was he a loser?

Six months later, Donie was back—but this time on a springboard, which is positioned just ten feet above the water. America's best male platform diver had been reborn as a top springboard competitor. In the 1996 Summer Olympics Donie placed fourth in the three meter springboard competition.

Donie didn't quit—he kept diving.

And any diver who hears the hollow pounding of his own fear in his ears and then returns to the water…that diver is a success.[1]

Defining *success* is a key component in swimming—and in discipleship.

The people you disciple *will* sin again—your investment of time and concern won't result in a perfect Christian who never fails. But you'll instill in those Christians a confidence that, when they sin, they can repent, be forgiven, and climb back into the pool.

The people you disciple *will* seldom appreciate the true importance of what you're teaching them…at least at that moment. It takes the crisis of an unexpected temptation before the impact of Bible memorization becomes obvious.

And the people you disciple may not even express gratitude. They may believe you're in the program for yourself because you enjoy meeting with someone who's supposed to listen to what you say.

Don't expect applause. Don't demand appreciation.

Just serve—and know that when you're faithful, a time will come

Chapter Eleven: Similar Temptations

[1] Sharon Robb, "Boca resident is first male diabetic to swim Channel," *Fort Lauderdale Sun Sentinel*, August 18, 1996, at http://72.14.203.104/search?q=cache:GcZb-mGLzncJ:www.usms.org/hist/sto/index.php%... Copyright © 1996-2006 United States Masters Swimming, Inc.

[2] Sharon Robb, "Diabetic swimmer likes the challenge of English Channel," *Fort Lauderdale Sun Sentinel*, August 10, 1996, at http://72.14.203.104/search?q=cache:GcZb-mGLzncJ:www.usms.org/hist/sto/index.php%... Copyright © 1996-2006 United States Masters Swimming, Inc.

[3] Ibid.

[4] Ibid.

Chapter Thirteen: Obedience

[1] George Barna, *Growing True Disciples* (Ventura, CA: The Barna Group, Ltd.) as mentioned in *The Barna Update*, "Discipleship Insights Revealed in New Book by George Barna," November 28, 2000, at http://www.barna.org/FlexPage.aspx?Page=BarnaUpdate&BarnaUpdateID=76

Chapter Fourteen: Becoming a Discipling Church

[1] Gerry Callahan, "Don't Look Now: Scott Donie, driven off the platform by nerves and depression, won the U.S. trials in the springboard," From the Magazine: *Sports Illustrated*, at http://sportsillustrated.cnn.com/events/1996/olympics/storyolympics/diving.html

Notes

Introduction
[1] D. Michael Lindsey, "Chapter 1, The Powerful Results of Church Satisfaction: *Analysis of Gallup Research," Friendship: Creating a Culture of Connectivity in your Church: New Gallup research with analysis by D. Michael Lindsey and ministry ideas from Group.* Loveland, CO: Group Publishing, Inc., 2005, pg10.

Chapter Two: Discipling Begins With You
[1] George Barna, *Growing True Disciples* (Ventura, CA: The Barna Group Ltd.), as mentioned in *The Barna Update*, "Discipleship Insights Revealed in New Book by George Barna," November 28, 2000, at http:www.barna.org/FlexPage.aspx?Page=BarnaUpdate&BarnaUpdateID=76

Chapter Seven: The Essential Discipline of Bible Study
[1] George Barna, *Growing True Disciples* (Ventura, CA: The Barna Group Ltd.) as mentioned in *The Barna Update*, "Discipleship Insights Revealed in New Book by George Barna," November 28, 2000, at http:www.barna.org/FlexPage.aspx?Page=BarnaUpdate&BarnaUpdateID=76

[2] Benjamin Franklin, *Poor Richard's Almanac*, 1757, as quoted in John Bartlett, *Familiar Quotations*, 10th ed, 1919, and cited in Bartleby.com's "Great Books Outline" at http://www.bartleby.com's "Great Books Outline" at http://www.bartleby.com/100/245.html

[3] Frank Newport, "Twenty-Eight Percent Believe Bible is Actual Word of God," *The Gallup Poll*, May 22, 2006, at http://poll.gallup.com/content/?ci=22885 Copyright © 2006 by the Gallup Organization, Princeton, NJ.

Chapter Ten: Three Months That Change Lives
[1] "Imprinting (psychology)," Wikipedia®, the free encyclopedia, a registered trademark of the Wikipedia Foundation, Inc., at http://en.wikipedia.org/wiki/Imprinting_(psychology) at 23:59, 30 June 2006.
[2] Ibid.
[3] Steven Pegram "Mark Spritz: And still the greatest swimming performance of all time," at http://www.usolympicteam.com/cfdocs/Munich/feature_spitz.cfm
[4] "Former IU Swim Coach Doc Counsilman Dies," at http://www.wishtv.com/globl/story.asp?s=1588106&ClientType=Printable Copyright © 2000-2006 WorldNow and WISH-TV

Tell the learner you'll let go—briefly. Gradually increase the amount of time the learner is floating without hanging onto you.

Have learners practice righting themselves in the water without your help. Have them push down against the water with their hands, lift their heads, and bring their legs forward in a knee bend before pushing their legs down toward the bottom of the pool. And it's important they *do all this at the same time.* Master that move and learners will be able to, in fairly shallow water, easily get upright without panic.

Proceed to practicing flutter kicking while holding the side of the pool. Ask learners to practice kicking while placing their faces in the water. Learners' tendency will be either to bend their knees too sharply (splashing lots of water!) or to keep their knees too stiff—which reduces power. While learners are holding the wall move their knees so they can feel what the proper amount of knee movement feels like.

While learners are standing, have them work on a free stroke. Ask learners bend over and stroke. Again—move their arms to the proper position while they practice putting their faces in the water and then breathe as they tilt their heads to the side. Beginners have a tendency to breathe by raising their heads up instead of to the side.

Add flutter kicking and stroking into the mix. Stay close by to provide counsel and safety.

Practice. Encourage. Lots.

A Summary:
How to Teach Someone To Swim

Be sure you know how to swim yourself. You can't teach what you don't know.

Develop a relationship of trust. This takes time—and can't be skipped.

Get in the water yourself first and then invite the learner in. Model the behavior you want to see.

Have the learner become familiar with the water. If it's a child, have the child jump up and down. For teenagers and adults, lightly splash them in the face.

Have the learner get his or her face in the water. Ask the learner to blow bubbles or to submerge and then stand up.

Pull the learner through the water. Take the learner's hands and pull him through the water. Take your time, the longer the pull, the more the learner will relax.

Have the learner put his or her face in the water as you pull the learner through the water. This step is where you find out if the learner trusts you.

when you complete the race and receive the ultimate fulfillment: a "well done, good and faithful servant" from the heart of the one who matters most.

It's all about not giving up.

If we don't give up, we can't lose.

Keep swimming.

FIRST STEPS

One-on-One Discipleship

Order a copy of the *First Steps* notebook from disciplinganother. com. This notebook will give you a practical tool for one-on-one discipleship.